Summer Reading

Summer Reading

Program and Evidence

Fay H. Shin

California State University, Long Beach

Stephen D. Krashen

University of Southern California

PEARSON

Boston • New York • San Francisco
Mexico City • Montreal • Toronto • London • Madrid • Munich • Paris
Hong Kong • Singapore • Tokyo • Cape Town • Sydney

Executive Editor: *Aurora Martínez Ramos*
Editorial Assistant: *Lynda Giles*
Marketing Manager: *Danae April*
Editorial-Production Service: *Publishers' Design & Production Services, Inc.*
Composition Buyer: *Linda Cox*
Manufacturing Buyer: *Linda Morris*
Electronic Composition and Interior Design: *Publishers' Design & Production Services, Inc.*
Cover Designer: *Kristina Mose-Libon*

For related titles and support materials, visit our online catalog at www.ablongman.com.

Between the time website information is gathered and then published, it is not unusual for some sites to have closed. Also, the transcription of URLs can result in typographical errors. The publisher would appreciate notification where these errors occur so that they may be corrected in subsequent editions.

ISBN-10: 0-205-50489-2
ISBN-13: 978-0-205-50489-3

Library of Congress Cataloging-in-Publication Data
Shin, Fay H.
    Summer reading : program and evidence / Fay H. Shin, Stephen D. Krashen.
      p. cm.
    Includes index.
    ISBN 0-205-50489-2 (alk. paper)
    1. Children—Books and reading—United States.   2. Reading promotion—United States.   3. Children's libraries—Activity programs—United States.
I. Krashen, Stephen D. II. Title.

    Z1037.A1S484 2008
    028.5'5—dc22

                                                    2007005632
Printed in the United States of America

Photo Credits: Page 1, T. Lindfors/Lindfors Photography; p. 27, Comstock Royalty Free Division; p. 65, Photodisc/Getty Images.

10 9 8 7 6 5 4 3 2 1   CST   11 10 09 08 07

For my daughters, Lauren and Chloe. They are, and always will be, my angels and inspiration.

Fay Shin

For the members of three glorious teams: Team Julian, Team Jordan, and Team Sidney.

Stephen Krashen

Contents

CHAPTER 2

The Summer Reading Program 27

What We Learned   65

Introduction

There has been wide recognition of importance of summer in literacy development, but it is not clear to educators what happens over the summer to affect literacy development or how to use the summer break.

Some have the view that all children "backslide" during summer. The research tells us that some children do, in fact, backslide, but others don't, and there are good reasons why this difference occurs: Children with access to books either hold their own or improve. Children without access to books do indeed backslide.

Summer school programs are typically aimed at children considered to be "behind" in reading, but usually attempt to continue the same kind of instruction done during the school year. Others recognize the importance and centrality of reading, but restrict students to certain texts (assigned reading lists) and provide little time to actually read.

We present here the results of a program that, we think, is fully consistent with the research on summer reading, as well as research on reading in general. The program was devoted to encouraging self-selected, enjoyable reading. We surrounded sixth graders with books we thought they would like, gave them time to browse and time to read, and tried to show that we cared about them and their reading. We also compared their progress in reading with students who did a "regular" summer program. The results were very encouraging.

This book is divided into three chapters. In the first chapter, we review research on what happens to literacy over the summer and why. In the second chapter, we present our program, and the results. In the final chapter, we summarize what we learned, the ideas we already had that were confirmed, and some new understandings about encouraging reading. We also include some appendices, which contain details for those interested in replicating our experiences, as well as a striking case history that we discovered after our manuscript was written.

Acknowledgments

This book and summer reading project would never have been possible without the support of many people.

First of all, we want to thank the coordinator and reading specialist, Kathleen Marshall. This program would have never been successful without her help, dedication, faith, and support. She always went the extra mile to ensure the success of the project because she knew this is what the students really needed.

Second, we want to thank all the summer school teachers for their cooperation and support: Eve Marin, Laurie Sierro, Sue Rogers, Laquita Williams, Danny Dunne, Kari Frazer, Clare Hanley, Clyde Hodge, Deanne Islas, Denise Rico. Their dedication and hard work made all of this happen.

Third, our "library coordinator," Winnie Llamera, who volunteered to help us when we needed her (which was every day). She was such a wonderful supporter and very dedicated to the community and students.

Fourth, thank you to those who gave insightful comments regarding the manuscript: Sheila Bostrom, Brush Schools, CO; Nancy Daniels, Helman Elementary School, OR; Mary Klink, Thomas Jefferson Elementary School, VA; and Erika Y. Tucker, Columbia Middle School, GA.

Lastly, we appreciate our research assistants who helped with collecting data (classroom observations, interviews, surveys): Jane Acoba, Tyler Post, Valerie Trede, Evangeline Ramos, Gayle Watkins, and Jennifer Warmerdam.

My Personal Thanks

I want to thank my husband, Ed, for all his help, advice, encouragement, and support while working on this project and throughout the years. He has always been my biggest supporter. Also, I want to thank my parents, Paul and Jung Shin—first for supporting me through my many years of education, and later for many hours of babysitting.

I would like to thank my friends, family, and colleagues who have supported me throughout the years in so many ways: Stephen Krashen, my co-author, mentor, advisor, and friend; Joan Wink, Robert Rueda, Simon Kim, Robert and Yoshiye Awaya, June Saruwatari, Ann Wong, Mandy Sabado, David and Sandy Shin, Annie Nguyen, Stan Jimbo, Kay Vongphoutone, Brenda Betts, and Kyungsook Cho.

I also want to thank the faculty and Teacher Education Department at California State University, Long Beach and California State University, Stanislaus for the opportunity to work on this project and book.

CHAPTER 1

What Happens over the Summer

"*T*he potential role of voluntary summer reading in closing the reading achievement gap has been neglected too long by educators, researchers, and policymakers."[1]

A Startling Finding

Children from high-income families do better in school and have more life success.

Anybody with any experience in education knows that children from high-income families do better in school than children from low-income families. They do better on standardized tests, are much more likely to stay in school, and are admitted to better colleges.[2] This advantage translates to life success; children of the wealthy are far more likely to become wealthy than children of the poor.[3]

Why do children from high-income families do better? Are their schools better and their teachers more talented? Do they get more help with their homework? Are they more motivated? Are they simply born smarter?

In at least one area, reading and literacy development, the results of some recent and some not-so-recent research strongly suggest that the difference between the achievement of children of high- and low-income families has little or nothing to do with what happens during the school year. The crucial time is the summer. Here is the startling result: Children from high- and low-income families appear to make similar gains in reading during the academic year. But children of poverty, however, fall behind in the summer, a little more each year, until the difference is huge.

Barbara Heyns found that most children make similar gains in reading during the school year. Children of poverty fall behind during the summer.

Barbara Heyns's Study

Barbara Heyns, a professor at New York University, has known about the effects of summer for nearly thirty years. Her book, *Summer Learning and the Effects of School*, was published in 1975. She studied seventh graders who lived in Atlanta in the spring of 1972. Some of the children were from high-income families and some were from low-income families. Let's look at her findings carefully—they are extremely important.[4]

Table 1.1 is from Heyns's book. It presents Heyns' data on vocabulary tests given to the children at the end of each school year, in the spring of 1971 and 1972, and the fall of 1971. Let's first see how much the children gained *during* the school year.

Heyns' table first gives us the national average, how much children throughout the United States gain in one school year. A comparison of fall 1971 with spring 1972 shows that the average gain in the United States for seventh graders was 0.7. This means seven months. (Notice that seventh graders in Atlanta did nearly as well, gaining 0.64 months during the school year.)

Table 1.1

Test of Word Knowledge

	Spring '71	Fall '71	Spring '72	School Gain	Summer Gain
National average	5.8	6.1	6.8	0.7	0.3
Atlanta	4.95	5	5.64	0.64	0.05
White					
Low income	5.8	5.47	6.27	0.8	–.33
High income	6.87	7.24	8	0.76	0.37
Black					
Low income	3.93	3.89	4.44	0.61	–.02
High income	5.2	5.57	6.45	0.88	0.37

Note: Numbers refer to grade level.

Source: Heyns (1975), table 3.2, p. 46.

Now let's look at the summer, the gain from spring 1971 to fall 1972. The national average is 0.3, or three months. Children in Atlanta, however, gained less than half of a month in vocabulary over the summer.

Notice that the average gain throughout the United States over a calendar year was exactly one year, as we would expect. But 30% of that growth occurred during the summer, when school was out.

The interesting comparison is between children of poverty and children from higher-income families. *Remarkably, both groups made similar gains in vocabulary during the academic year.* From fall 1971 to spring 1972, white children from high-income families gained 0.76 months, and white children from low-income families gained eight months. (The results for African American children are, however, somewhat different: The low-income group gained six months; the highest gained somewhat more, a little less than nine months, a three-month difference.)

But now consider what happened during the summer, by looking at the scores from spring 1971 to fall 1971. Both low-socioeconomic status (SES) groups did poorly compared to the high-SES groups. The low-income white children actually lost three months during the summer, while the high-income white children gained nearly four months. In fact, this data shows that about half of the total gain made by the high-SES group took place during the summer.

The data for African American children is similar: Scores for low-SES children were stagnant over the summer, while higher-SES children gained nearly four months, the same gain as the higher-SES white children. Again, nearly half the gains made by the higher-SES children occurred during the summer.

The Cumulative Effect

The summer advantage is cumulative, that is, every summer and over time it gets larger and larger, until the difference between high family income and low family income children is gigantic.

The summer effect is cumulative: After a few years, the difference between children from high- and low-income families is enormous.

Table 1.2 is from Entwisle, Alexander, and Olson's book, *Children, Schools and Inequality*. This book was published 22 years after Heyns's book. The data comes from a different city, Baltimore. Reading comprehension test results are reported, and three groups were studied (high, mid, and low family income) rather than two. Despite the studies' differences, the results are the same.[5]

Table 1.2

The Cumulative Difference

Reading Comprehension: Baltimore City Schools

School Year	Low Income	Mid Income	High Income
Year 1	56.7	68.6	60.8
Year 2	48	45.4	40.1
Year 3	31.2	35.6	33.7
Year 4	33.1	41	31.7
Year 5	24.3	29.1	24.6
Total Gain	193.3	219.7	190.9
Summer			
Year 1	−3.7	−2.1	15
Year 2	−3.5	1.8	8.5
Year 3	1.6	2.5	14.9
Year 4	4.5	1.6	10.4
Year 5	1.9	−4.1	−2.2
Total Gain	0.8	−0.3	46.6

Year 1 = end of first grade

Source: Entwisle, Alexander, and Olson (1997), table 3.1, p. 34.

The top part of the table shows gains in reading comprehension test scores during the school year for five consecutive years, following the same group of children, starting in grade one. Just as Heyns showed, there is little difference among the groups. If we look at the row marked "total gain," we see that the children from the highest and lowest income families gained nearly the exact same number of total points in reading during the school year, with the middle group doing only slightly better.

But now look at the bottom half of the table. The children from high-income families made consistently better gains in reading over the summer, and at the end of five years they were far ahead of children from both groups.

What Causes the Difference over the Summer? READING

Children from high-income families do more free voluntary reading over the summer.

If free reading is the explanation for summer gains, it shows that children can improve from pleasure reading alone.

There is a simple explanation for these differences: Reading. Children from wealthier families read more over the summer. They do more *free voluntary reading,* or recreational reading, or just plain reading for fun. And they read more because they have more access to books.

If this explanation is true, it shakes the foundations of education in the language arts. It says that children can become better readers and improve their vocabulary without school, on their own. It says that all the drills and exercises and workbooks are not necessary.

Before jumping to conclusions, however, let's take a closer look at the research. We start by taking another look at Barbara Heyns's important study. Heyns investigated children's reading habits and found that the number of books children said they read over the summer was a significant predictor of how they did on the vocabulary test given in the fall.

An extremely important feature of Heyns's analysis is that it took many other predictors of reading scores into consideration: We know from previous studies (and common sense) that children who score higher on a vocabulary test in the spring will also score higher in fall, and we know that children from higher-income families and families with better educated parents generally do better on these tests. Heyns used a sophisticated statistical technique (called multiple regression) that "controlled" for these factors, that is, it measured the impact of how many books the children said they read that was free of the influence of other factors. In a sense, it allowed us to pretend that all children did equally well on the spring test and came from similar families. Heyns's study, in other words, makes it clear that the amount of recreational reading the children did was a real cause of gains over the summer.

We had to wait nearly 30 years for a replication of Heyns's results. Jimmy Kim of Harvard University found very similar results, examining test scores and reading habits of a group of sixth graders. Once again, those who read more over the summer did better on a reading test given in the fall. Like Heyns, Kim used multiple regression to control for other factors that could influence reading scores. In addition to controlling for those Heyns did, he also controlled for gender, ethnicity, the children's attitudes toward reading, and whether the child was emotionally disturbed, learning disabled, or a speaker of English as a second language. Once again, we can be confident that the amount of recreational reading done was a real influence on how much children improved in reading over the summer.[6]

Many people want to know how much reading a child has to do to make an impact. This would be good to know; it would give us an idea of how many books we need to provide. Kim estimated that reading five books over the summer results in a gain of about three percentiles (normal curve equivalents) on

Barbara Heyns's study controlled for other factors that could account for gains in literacy over the summer. This makes it clear that free reading was the cause of the gains.

Jimmy Kim also found that more summer reading means better gains in literacy.

....

*Kim reported
that, on average,
reading five
books over the
summer means a
three percentile
gain on
standardized
tests.*

....

standardized reading tests. That's a large impact. Consider what would happen with an additional ten books over the summer, continued for seven years: a gain of 42 percentiles, easily enough to account for the difference in reading scores between children from low-income families and the children of the high-income families. (Of course, Kim's figure is imprecise—books vary quite a bit in size and complexity, but Kim's results give us a rough idea.)

Celano and Neuman (2001) compared the reading ability of 105 children from low-income families who regularly attended summer library programs, and 89 children who went to summer camps that were located near the libraries.[7] The library programs "offered several special events as well as the usual gifts and giveaways for reading a certain number of books. Librarians at both locations were among the city's best, offering years of experience along with enthusiasm for helping children from needy areas" (pp. 41–42). The summer camps "featured normal activities for summer camp programs—swimming, arts and crafts, field trips—but no reading programs of any sort" (p. 42).

Children who attended the library regularly did better than the summer camp children on two measures of literacy: The grade level of both groups was third grade but the summer readers, according to the Johns Reading Inventory Test, read at level 2.9, while the summer camp children read at the 2.2 level. The children also took author and title recognition tests, which measure how familiar children are with different children's book authors and titles. Performance on tests such as these have been shown to correlate with reading ability and reading habits.[8] The summer readers did much better, recognizing 6 authors out of 25, compared to only 3 for the summer camp children, and 10 titles, compared to only 5 for the summer camp children. Of course, it could be the case that parents of children who show more interest in reading are more likely to send the children to a reading program rather than a camp, but the results are clearly consistent with other studies that show positive effects for summer reading.

The idea that reading more over the summer results in better reading achievement is of course not an exotic idea. It agrees not only with common sense but also with a vast research literature: One of the best-established findings in all of educational research is that recreational reading is good for literacy development.

A number of studies confirm that students who participate in in-school self-selected recreational reading programs, such as sustained silent reading (SSR), make at least as much progress in reading as those in regular language arts programs, and usually do better, especially if the programs last for an academic year or longer, that is, if the students do enough reading.

The results of many other studies show that free voluntary reading results in gains in literacy.

Hooked on Books

The event that started current interest in in-school free reading in the United States was the publication, in 1965, of Daniel Fader's *Hooked on Books*, a book that nearly achieved best-seller status. Fader described how he and his colleagues assembled a truly "print-rich" environment consisting of genuinely interesting reading material for a group known to be resistant to reading: reform-school boys aged 12 to 17, boys labeled as juvenile delinquents.[9]

Fader and his colleagues surrounded the boys with interesting books and magazines they knew the boys were interested in. They vastly simplified library procedures—the boys were each given a paperback book and told they could return it anytime and get another book in exchange. There were no overdue fines and no book reports.

It worked. Over a two-year period, the boys read an average of one book every other day. This was not assigned reading and they received no rewards. They read simply because the books were interesting and they were available.

The Hooked on Books program worked with reform school boys.

*In-class self-
selected reading,
or sustained
silent reading,
has been a
consistent winner
in research done
all over the
world.*

Fader's colleague, Elton McNeil, kept track of the boys' reading progress and compared them to similar boys who were not participating in the Hooked on Books program. The Hooked on Books boys made superior progress on tests of reading comprehension, writing complexity, and writing fluency. They were also clearly involved with the reading; McNeil noted that while watching their school team during basketball games, the Hooked on Books boys were not always watching the game; they were often seen reading their books.

At the time of this writing, approximately 60 evaluations of in-school free reading have been published, studies in which children and teenagers who are given time to do free reading in school are compared with similar students who spend a similar amount of time in "regular instruction." Reading emerges a clear winner in this research. And the findings are the same no matter where in the world it is done. We will spare you all 60 studies, but cannot resist sharing a few.

Warwick Elley: The Fiji Island Study

Fader's *Hooked on Books* is certainly the pioneering study, but Warwick Elley's study has had the most impact worldwide. Warwick Elley is a genuine hero in the world of education. Now a retired university professor, Elley has had a distinguished career, serving the profession in many ways.

In 1983, Elley and his colleague Francis Mangubhai published a paper that is, in our view, one of the most remarkable ever done in the field of education. If education had a Nobel Prize, Elley and Mangubhai would have won it. The paper was published in the flagship journal of the International Reading Association, the *Reading Research Quarterly*, considered the most prestigious journal in the world today in reading and literacy development.[10]

In the Fiji Islands, English is taught as a foreign language, beginning in kindergarten, for 30 minutes a day. Elley and Mangubhai looked at the progress of fourth and fifth graders, who were divided into three different groups for their English class.

One group received the standard curriculum, a version of the "audio-lingual" method. Most readers have experienced something like this method. It includes drills, with students repeating what teachers say, explicit grammar instruction, and the correction of students' errors.

A second group had sustained silent reading: They spent the entire 30-minute English class reading storybooks on their own. There were no book reports, no tests, and no accountability. It should be pointed out that these children had, by then, several years of English instruction and the reading was comprehensible for them.

A third group had a program called "Shared Book Experience," which is quite similar to what is known in the United States as "Big Books." The children were read to from oversized books, which the teacher held so that the children could follow the story as it was being read. This was followed by discussion and other literature activities.

Elley and Mangubhai presented the results of tests of reading comprehension given to all three groups. The differences were spectacular. Children in the audio-lingual (traditional instruction) group made the least gains: fourth graders gained 6.5 months on the reading test the first year, fifth graders only 2.5 months. Those who were in the free reading group did far better—the fourth graders gained 15 months and the fifth graders gained 9 months. And all they did was read! The Shared Reading group also did extremely well: Both fourth and fifth graders gained 15 months over the year.

The second year of the project, both reading groups (SSR and Shared Reading) performed equivalently, and pulled even farther ahead of the audio-lingual group. Gains were not limited to tests of

Elley and Mangubhai provided very convincing evidence for the power of reading for children studying English in the Fiji Islands.

reading comprehension. The readers also did better on tests of listening, writing, and grammar.

In our view, this stunning result should have changed the entire world of language education immediately: It satisfied all the requirements for a scientific study, appeared in a highly rated journal, and was performed by respected scholars.

Elley replicated this result in another major study, this time done in Singapore, and it was published in another top-rated professional journal, *Language Learning*, in 1991.[11]

Beniko Mason: Osaka, Japan

Let's look at one more study, just to emphasize that the kinds of results Elley got occur in very different surroundings. Beniko Mason is responsible for much of the popularity of in-school recreational reading in English classes in Japan and her influence has spread to other countries as well. Her first contribution to this field occurred when she was teaching a required English class to first-year students in a women's college in Osaka, Japan. Mason developed a reading comprehension test that she regularly gave to her students at the beginning and the end of each academic year, and found that using traditional instruction her students made modest progress over the year. Her entry into the field of recreational reading began when she was assigned a group of problem students, students who had been unsuccessful in English and who had dropped or failed English class numerous times. They were called *retakers*, or *Sei Rishu* in Japanese.[12]

Mason realized after a short time that the usual curriculum was not going to work with these students. She threw it out and substituted her own version of in-school recreational reading, which she called *extensive reading*. Students read from graded readers, that is, books written especially for students of English as a second language. Students were encouraged to begin with very easy readers, well below their level, and gradually moved on to harder books, with some reading easy authentic texts (books written by and for native speakers of English) toward the end of the semester. The entire class period was devoted to reading. Students were only asked to write a very short comment on what they read in Japanese.

The results were gratifying: On the reading comprehension test, the retakers started well below the regular students, but by the end of the semester, they had nearly caught up. Also, they said they liked this English class a lot better than other English classes they had taken in the past.

What we can safely conclude from the research is that recreational reading works: It works in first language and second language, it works for children, teenagers and adults, and it works in every country in which it has been tried. All that is required for in-school free reading to work is a plentiful supply of interesting and comprehensible reading material and a quiet place to read.[13]

Sustained silent reading succeeded with very reluctant college students in Osaka, Japan.

Why Some Children Read More: Access to Books

There is an obvious reason why children from higher-income families read more over the summer: They have far more access to books, and more access to books means more reading.

There has always been a great deal of discussion in the field of reading about how to encourage children to read; there are debates on whether we should give children incentives (rewards) for reading, whether we should deliberately push students to read, whether we should use read-alouds and author visits, and so on. But one factor has been seriously neglected, until recently: the overwhelming role of access to books. A number of studies indicate that given access to books

The important factor of access to books has been overlooked.

*Debra Von
Sprecken found
that nearly all
students actually
read during SSR
time, if you
observe them
during the middle
of the school
year.*

*Research
suggests that
many reluctant
readers may
become
enthusiastic
readers when
given more
access to
interesting
reading material.*

that are interesting and comprehensible, nearly all children and teenagers will read.

Debra Von Sprecken, while a graduate student at the University of Southern California, observed middle-school students during sustained silent reading time and concluded that 90% of the children were actually reading. (We should point out that the observations took place in the middle of the school year; during the first few weeks of SSR much less reading takes place—it takes a while for children to find books that are right for them.[14])

In fact, what we call reluctant readers are, most of the time, simply children with little access to books. This was confirmed by University of Texas researchers Jo Worthy and Sharon McKool, who interviewed eleven sixth graders who "hated to read." Nine of the 11 reluctant readers had little access to interesting reading material at home, in the school library, or in their classroom libraries, and none had visited the public library in the year before the interview.[15]

The two students who had access to interesting reading were the only two "who read with any degree of regularity" (p. 252). Ironically, even though all were described as reluctant readers, all appeared to be quite enthusiastic about some kinds of reading, especially "light reading" (e.g., comics and the "Goosebumps" series).

Very similar results were reported by San Francisco State University researcher Christy Lao. Lao asked college students studying to become public school teachers about their reading habits when they were younger. All 12 who described themselves as reluctant readers when young said they grew up in print-poor environments. All 10 who described themselves as enthusiastic early readers said they grew up surrounded by lots of books.[16]

As impressive as this data is, there is one obvious fact staring us in the face that demonstrates that children will read if interesting books are available: the spectacular success of the Harry Potter books.

Access to books does not guarantee reading. Some children will not read even if they are surrounded by good books. Researcher Sam Pack, for example, described a group of what he called "library latchkey" children, children whose parents used the public library as a "free source of after-school care" from one to six hours per day. Some of the children, despite the presence of so many books, never read any of them, but spent their time on the computer, or simply "hanging out" with the other children.[17]

But these children are in the minority. Given access to interesting, comprehensible books, most children will read. This means that the first priority in any literacy campaign is making sure children have access to books. This is not a trivial task: Many children, unfortunately, have little access to interesting reading material.[18]

Poor Children Have Very Little Access to Books

The difference in access to reading material between children of poverty and children of the middle class is enormous. Let us review just three of the heartbreaking studies that have recently appeared that show this.

The Watts/Beverly Hills Study

Stephen Krashen was a participant in one of the three studies, but he played third fiddle. The investigators who really deserve the credit were Courtney Smith and Rebecca Constantino. Smith and Constantino examined the availability of books in two very different California communities, affluent Beverly Hills and high-poverty Watts.[19]

We first asked children in Beverly Hills and Watts how many books they had in their home that were available to them, books of their own or books owned by brothers and sisters that they could read. The average

The first priority in any literacy campaign is to provide access to interesting reading material.

Children in low-income Watts had much less access to books in school, at home, and in their communities than children in high-income Beverly Hills.

number in Beverly Hills was 200. This may seem like a lot, but this is not unusual for middle-class children. The average number for children in Watts was less than one, actually 0.4 books per household.

School, we found, did not level the playing field. In fact, school made the situation worse. We examined classroom libraries: Those in schools in Beverly Hills had an average of 400 books, but those in Watts averaged only 50. The average Beverly Hills child had four times as many books at home as were found in the entire average classroom library in Watts! We also found that the school libraries in Beverly Hills had two to three times as many books as those in Watts, and the public libraries were also far better. The average child in Beverly Hills we interviewed could walk to five bookstores; the average child in Watts could walk to only one bookstore.

Neuman and Celano

Public libraries in high-income communities have better collections, are open longer hours, and have far better children's books sections.

Susan Neuman and Donna Celano's landmark study was very thorough and, in addition to replicating our findings, found new inequalities. They compared access to books and to print in general in two middle-class communities and two high-poverty communities. In the wealthy communities, there was more readable, legible print in their neighborhood (e.g., ads, signs), and more places where one could see people reading in public. The school libraries in the middle-class communities had certified librarians, but in the low-income communities they were staffed by part-time help. The public libraries in the middle-class communities were open during the evenings, but this was not so in the low-income communities.[20]

There was also a huge difference in the availability of books in bookstores. For those in low-income areas, the only books available in stores were children's books in drugstores. But children of middle-class families had access to several well-stocked bookstores, which had magnificent collections of children's and adolescent literature.

Neuman and Celano concluded that "children in middle-income neighborhoods were likely to be deluged with a wide variety of reading materials. However, children from poor neighborhoods would have to aggressively and persistently seek them out" (p. 15).

Di Loreto and Tse: Santa Fe Springs

Christina Di Loreto and Lucy Tse's study adds to the dismal picture. They examined the children's section of the Bevery Hills public library and the public library in working class Sante Fe Springs, California.

The Beverly Hills library contained 60,000 children's books, two for every child in the community; the Santa Fe Springs library only had 13,000, less than one for each child in the community. The Beverly Hills children's section subscribed to 30 children's magazines, while the Santa Fe Springs had subscriptions to 20. The Santa Fe Springs library had no staff dedicated exclusively to the children's section; in Beverly Hills there were 12 staff members working in the children's section.[21]

More Access to Books Results in More Reading

Study after study show that children who read more grow up in homes with more books.[22] We also know that children read more when there are more books available to them in their classroom libraries[23] and when there are more books available to them in their school libraries.[24]

*A series of
studies by Keith
Curry Lance and
colleagues shows
that the better
the school
library, the
higher the
reading scores.*

*The public
library is the
major source of
reading material
for children of
poverty during
the summer.
Both Heyns and
Kim found that
more access to
the public
library during
the summer
resulted in more
reading.*

Better Libraries Mean Better Reading!

If children get a good percentage of their books from libraries, and more access means more reading and better reading, we would expect to find that the better the school library, the higher the reading scores. Keith Curry Lance, working for the State of Colorado, found exactly that. Elementary schools in Colorado that had better school libraries (more books, more staffing, and the presence of a certified librarian) had higher reading scores (Lance used the same kinds of statistical techniques that Barbara Heyns and Jimmy Kim did to neutralize the effect of poverty and other potential contributors to reading test scores.[25])

Access to Books during the Summer

Children of poverty have only one source of books available to them during the summer: the public library. Interestingly, the scholars we met earlier who studied the impact of summer reading also studied the impact of having access to a public library. Barbara Heyns, in her 1975 book, tells us that children who used the public library more, read more (those who reported using the library regularly read 6.2 books over the summer, those who did not read 3.9). But of greater interest is the fact that those who lived closer to the library read more: Those who lived under seven blocks from the library averaged 5.7 books read over the summer, while those who lived seven blocks or more from the library averaged 5.1 books.

Nearly 30 years later, Jimmy Kim found the same thing: In his study there was a strong relationship between the amount of reading done over the summer by fifth graders and whether students said it was easy to access books at a library. And once again, other research confirms the importance of children having access to a good public library. A reluctant reader studied by Christy Lao who had grown up in a home with very few books became a reader thanks to the public library. In the fourth grade, she discovered Judy Blume's books, and her reading, she said, "took off from there" (p. 16).

Pulling It All Together

Let's now pull this all together. Here is what we have established:

1. In general, children from higher-income families do a lot better in school. Among other things, they do better on tests of reading and vocabulary.

2. The importance of summer. The difference we see in how well children read, as well as their growth in vocabulary, appears to be heavily influenced by what happens over the summer. Studies show that children of the poor and children of higher-income families show similar growth over the school year; children from higher-income families, however, make much more progress over the summer. Over time, the contribution of summer reading growth appears to be enough to account for the difference in performance on reading tests between these two groups of children.

3. The crucial activity that occurs during the summer, the activity that causes the difference in growth in literacy, is recreational reading. Children from higher-income families read more over the summer.

4. The reason middle-class children read more over the summer is that they have more access to books. They have more access to books at home, live closer to bookstores, and live closer to public libraries. Also, public libraries available to the children from high-income families are better. They have more books, more staff, and are open longer hours.

5. Other research confirms that children read more when they have more access to books.

6. Other research also confirms that children who read more, read better, and show better development of vocabulary, writing, and grammar.

7. Research also confirms that children of the poor have little access to books in general.

This summary leads us to an inevitable and simple conclusion: Children of poverty need more access to reading material. And as Jeff McQuillan has pointed out, it doesn't matter where they get their reading: It can come from school, home, or the public library.[26]

We close this section with one more confirmation of the importance of access to print: Emery and Csikszentmihalyi (1982) compared 15 men of blue-collar background who became college professors with 15 men of very similar background who grew up to become blue-collar workers. The future professors lived in a much more print-rich environment and did far more reading when they were young. All of them came from low-income families—but one group had access to print and took advantage of it.[27]

$\mathcal{N}$OTES

1. Richard Allington and Anne McGill-Franzen, The impact of summer setback on the reading achievement gap. *Phi Delta Kappan* 85(1)(2003), 68–75.

2. In research studies socioeconomic status (SES), whether measured by family income, parent education, or parent occupation, is usually the most powerful predictor of achievement, sometimes outweighing all other factors. Karl White, The relation between socioeconomic status and academic achievement. *Psychological Bulletin* 91(1982), 461–81.

3. Simonton (1994) documents this in detail: In one study of eminent scientists, "not one came from a family where the chief breadwinner was an

unskilled laborer, and only 3% had fathers who were skilled workers. In contrast, 53% were the sons of professional men . . . those who managed to get Nobel laureates are nearly twice as likely to have fathers who were professionals, managers, or proprietors. On the leadership side, a similar pattern holds. In the United States, for example, the log cabin myth is just that, pure myth. Between 1789 and 1934, 58% of the presidents, vice-presidents, and cabinet secretaries had fathers who were professionals, officials, or proprietors; only 4% of the fathers were wage earners, and 38% were farmers . . . the same socioeconomic edge may be witnessed in endeavors beyond creativity or leadership. For instance, the top chess players of the world are most likely to emerge from homes where one or both parents enjoyed a university education. . . . Those studies that have examined a fuller range of achievement endeavors have found similar disparities. Of more than 300 contemporary creators, leaders, and celebrities, 80% emanated from business or professional home, while only 6% ascended from dire poverty." Dean Keith Simonon, *Greatness: Who Makes History and Why* (New York: Guilford Press, 1994), p. 157.

4. Barbara Heyns, *Summer Learning and the Effect of School* (New York: Academic Press, 1975).
5. Doris Entwisle, Karl Alexander, and Linda Olson, *Children, Schools, and Inequality* (Boulder, CO: Westview Press, 1997).
6. Jimmy Kim, Summer reading and the ethnic achievement gap. *Journal of Education for Students Placed at Risk* 9(2)(2003), 169–88.
7. Donna Celano and Susan Neuman, *The Role of Public Libraries in Children's Literacy Development* (Harrisburg, PA: Pennsylvania Library Association, 2001).
8. James Cipielewski and Keith Stanovich, Assessing print exposure and orthographic processing skill in children: A quick measure of reading experience. *Journal of Educational Psychology* 82(1990), 733–40; Linda Allen, J. Cipielewski, and Keith Stanovich, Multiple indicators of children's reading habits and attitudes: Construct validity and cognitive correlates. *Journal of Educational Psychology* 9(84)(1992), 489–503.

9. *Hooked on Books* first appeared in 1965, and underwent several revisions. To our knowledge, the most recent is: Daniel Fader, *The New Hooked on Books* (New York: Berkeley Books, 1976).

10. Warwick Elley and Francis Mangubhai, The impact of reading on second language learning. *Reading Research Quarterly* 19(1983), 53–67.

11. Warwick Elley, Acquiring literacy in a second language: The effect of book-based programs. *Language Learning* 41(1991), 375–411.

12. Beniko Mason and Stephen Krashen, Extensive reading in English as a foreign language. *System* 25(1997), 91–102.

13. Results from other areas of research also support the "reading hypothesis." There are compelling case histories of people who made remarkable gains in literacy through self-selected reading alone (Krashen, 2004). In addition, several studies show that readers can gain a small but reliable amount of vocabulary and spelling knowledge by reading an unfamiliar word in a comprehensible context only one time. Given enough reading, this small increment can account for adult vocabulary size (Nagy, Herman, and Anderson, 1985; Swanborn and de Glopper, 1999). Finally, correlational studies similar to those carried out by Heyns and Kim also show that those who read more, read better (Krashen, 2003). William Nagy, Patricia Herman, and Richard Anderson, Learning words from context. *Reading Research Quarterly* 23(1985), 6–50; M.S.L. Swanborn and K. de Glopper, Incidental word learning while reading: A meta-analysis. *Review of Educational Research* 69(3)(1999), 261–85; Stephen Krashen, *Explorations in Language Acquisition and Use: The Taipei Lectures* (Portsmouth, NH: Heinemann, 2003); Stephen Krashen, *The Power of Reading* (Westport, CT: Libraries Unlimited; Portsmouth, NH: Heinemann, 2004).

14. Debra Von Sprecken and Stephen Krashen, Do students read during sustained silent reading? *California Reader* 32(1)(1998), 11–13. Two other studies have confirmed our results. Kera Cohen wanted to know whether our results were influenced by the fact that the observers were in the room with the children: The children might have realized they

were being watched and read more than usual. Cohen observed eighth graders "unobtrusively," making sure that they did not know they were being observed, over a two-week period: 94% were reading during SSR. She noted that enthusiasm for sustained silent reading was not high at the beginning of the school year, but increased after a month or two for nearly all students. In another study, Herda and Ramos (2001) reported that 63% of students observed in SSR sessions in grades 1 through 12 were actively reading; in grades 1 through 5, the percentages were much higher, ranging from 76% to 100%. In the upper grades, students were given the option of studying or pleasure reading, and a substantial percentage took advantage of the study option. Nevertheless, quite a few students were reading for pleasure, ranging from 29% in grade 12 to 65% in grade nine. Kera Cohen, Reluctant eighth grade readers enjoy sustained silent reading. *California Reader* 33(1)(1999), 22–25; Rene Herda and Francis Ramos, How consistently do students read during sustained silent reading? *California School Library Journal* 24(2)(2001), 29–31.

15. Jo Worthy and Sharon McKool, Students who say they hate to read: The importance of opportunity, choice, and access. In D. Leu, C. Kinzer, and K. Hinchman (eds.), *Literacies for the 21st Century: Research and Practice* (Chicago: National Reading Conference, 1996), pp. 245–56.
16. Christy Lao, Prospective teachers' journey to becoming readers. *New Mexico Journal of Reading* 32(2)(2003), 14–20.
17. Sam Pack, Public library use, school performance, and the parental X-factor: A bio-documentary approach to children's snapshots. *Reading Improvement* 37(2000), 161–72.
18. Contrary to popular opinion, most children like to read, and also contrary to popular opinion, there is no clear evidence that there is a marked decline in interest in reading as children get older (Stephen Krashen and Debra Von Sprecken, Is there a decline in the reading romance? *Knowledge Quest* 30(3)(2002), 11–17). The READ California survey confirmed, for example, that teenagers like to read. The poll surveyed 201 subjects between ages 10 and

17. Sixty-four percent of the respondents rated reading 7 or better on a scale of 1 to 10, where 1 = not fun and 10 = a lot of fun. Thirty-six percent agreed that reading is "really cool" and another 55% agreed that reading is "kind of cool," a total of 91% of the sample. Teenagers also appreciated the value of reading: 99% felt that reading skill was "really important" (88%) or "kind of important" (11%) for success in the future. (Fairbank, Maslin, Maullin and Associates, *California Statewide Poll*, Job #620-157. Santa Monica, CA: California Opinion Research, 1999).

19. Courtney Smith, Rebecca Constantino, and Stephen Krashen, Differences in print environment for children in Beverly Hills, Compton and Watts. *Emergency Librarian* 24(4)(1996), 4–5. (We also examined the print environment in Compton, California, but do not include it here.)

20. Susan Neuman and Donna Celano, Access to print in low-income and middle-income communities. *Reading Research Quarterly* 36(1)(2001), 8–26.

21. Christina Di Loreto and Lucy Tse, Seeing is believing: Disparity in books in two Los Angeles area public libraries. *School Library Quarterly* 17(3)(1999), 31–36.

22. Stephen Krashen, *The Power of Reading* (Westport, CT: Libraries Unlimited; Portsmouth, NH: Heinemann, 2004); Christy Lao, Prospective teachers' journey to becoming readers. *New Mexico Journal of Reading* 32(2)(2003), 14–20.

23. Morrow and Weinstein (1982) reported that installing well-designed library corners in kindergarten classes that previously did not have them resulted in more use of books and other "literature activities" by children during free playtime. In addition, children did more free reading when the books in the library corner were more physically accessible, when they were within the children's reach, and when teachers allowed the children to take books home from the classroom library (Morrow, 1982). Lesley Morrow, Home and school correlates of early interest in literature. *Journal of Educational Research* 75(1983), 339–44; Lesley Morrow and Carol Weinstein, Increasing children's use of literature through program and physical changes. *Elementary School Journal* 83(1982), 131–37.

24. We have known this for a long time: Cleary (1939) reported that children in a school with no school library averaged 3.8 books read over a four-week period, while children from a school with a school library averaged exactly double that figure, 7.6 books. Gaver (1963) reported that children who had access to school libraries did more reading than children who only had access to centralized book collections (without librarians), who in turn read more than children who only had access to class-room collections. In a study of libraries and reading in 41 states and the District of Columbia, McQuillan (1998) also found that better school libraries (those with more books) resulted in more reading by students. Students take more books out of school libraries that have more books and stay open longer (Houle and Montmarquette, 1984). McQuillan and Au (2001) reported that high school students did more reading when their teachers took them to the school library on planned library visits more often. One of Lao's (2003) "enthusiastic" readers reports that her parents were avid readers and read to her, but books were not plentiful at home. Linda tells us that her mother got books from other sources, such as the public library, and that the school library was especially important in her life: "My school library was like a second home. I was always there and loved to read." Florence Cleary, Why children read. *Wilson Library Bulletin* 14(1939), 119–26; Mary Gaver, *Effectiveness of Centralized Library Service in Elementary Schools* (New Brunswick, NJ: Rutgers University Press, 1963); Rachel Houle and Claude Montmarquette, An empirical analysis of loans by school libraries. *Alberta Journal of Educational Research* 30(1984), 104–14; Christy Lao, Prospective teachers' journey to becoming readers. *New Mexico Journal of Reading* 32(2)(2003), 14–20; Jeff McQuillan, *The Literacy Crisis: False Claims and Real Solutions* (Portsmouth, NH: Heinemann, 1998); Jeff McQuillan and Julie Au, The effect of print access on reading frequency. *Reading Psychology* 22(2001), 225–48.

25. Lance and his colleagues have replicated their results in Colorado and in other states. Keith Lance, Lynda Welborn, and Christine Hamilton-Pennell, *The Impact of School Library Media Centers on Academic Achievement* (Castle Rock, CO: Hi Willow Research

and Publishing, 1993); Keith Lance, Christine Hamilton-Pennell, Marcia Rodney, Lois Petersen, and Clara Sitter, *Information Empowered: The School Librarian as an Academic Achievement in Alaska Schools* (Juno, AK: Alaska State Library, 1999); Keith Lance, Marcia Rodney, and Christine Hamilton-Pennell, *How School Librarians Help Kids Achieve Standards: The Second Colorado Study* (San Jose: Hi Willow Research and Publishing, 2000); Keith Lance, Marcia Rodney, and Christine Hamilton-Pennell, *Measuring to Standards: The Impact of School Library Programs and Literacy in Pennsylvania Schools* (Greensburg, PA: Pennsylvania Citizens for Better Libraries, 2000). Other researchers have found similar results. Both McQuillan and Krashen reported a clear relationship between the quality of school libraries and performance on the NAEP reading test for fourth graders for the 41 states in the United States that administered the NAEP. McQuillan reported a very strong relationship between the overall print environment (school library, public library, books in the home and NAEP scores ($r = .68$), and this relationship remained strong even when the effect of poverty was considered. Elley (1992) surveyed reading achievement in 32 countries and found that the quality of a country's school libraries was a significant predictor of its rank in reading. Stephen Krashen, School libraries, public libraries, and the NAEP reading scores. *School Library Media Quarterly* 23(1995), 235–38; Jeff McQuillan, *The Literacy Crisis: False Claims and Real Solutions* (Portsmouth, NH: Heinemann, 1998); Warwick Elley, *How in the World Do Students Read?* (Hamburg: International Association for the Evaluation of Educational Achievement, 1992).

26. Jeff McQuillan, *The Literacy Crisis: False Claims and Real Solutions* (Portsmouth, NH: Heinemann, 1998).

27. Olga Emery and Mihaly Csikszentmihalyi, The socialization effects of cultural role models in ontogenetic development and upward mobility. *Child Psychiatry and Human Development* 12(1982), 3–19.

CHAPTER 2

The Summer Reading Program

*The usual
approach to
summer reading
emphasizes
"skills," not free
voluntary
reading.*

*Our approach to
summer reading
included a "book
flood" and giving
children time to
read.*

*T*he idea of providing help in reading is certainly not new. In fact, newspapers regularly report on "reading camps" for children. But few reading camps make recreational reading the core. Some programs include some free reading, but nearly always provide children incentives (rewards) for reading, a practice with no support in the research.[1]

The summer camps we have read about also focus heavily on skill-building, the direct teaching of phonics, vocabulary and grammar. Some direct teaching has value, but the impact of this teaching is very limited: As we saw in chapter one, the primary means of the development of these literacy "skills" is reading itself.[2]

In this chapter we describe what we did and what progress the students made. We created an intensive reading program—a Reading Camp, but with a focus on independent reading. We also created a "book flood," supplying children with a large quantity of books. And we gave the children time to read: More than half of the classroom time was spent on independent reading. In other words, The Summer Reading Program was very different from the usual reading camps.

Some Predictions

Our project was also a scientific experiment. When you do an experiment you test a hypothesis; you make a prediction and you see if the results confirm your prediction. We began with these hypotheses:

> *Students will improve.* By providing students with access to high-interest reading materials and by allowing students an opportunity for self-selected reading, students will improve their reading ability and improve their knowledge of vocabulary. It is not enough, however, to show that students get better. One could argue that students will probably get better in reading with any reading program. We need a stronger hypothesis.

Students will improve more than comparisons. It is important to compare the students' progress to those who received a regular program over the summer. This will tell us how efficient our approach was. The comparison students should be similar to those in Goosebumps summer in all ways: they should come from similar homes, have similar access to reading outside of school, and should differ only in what they did in summer school.[3]

Attitudes toward reading will improve. It doesn't really matter how much students improve in reading if they don't continue reading after the program ends. And they will continue reading if they like it, and if they have access to books. We therefore decided to investigate whether attitudes toward reading improved. In other words, will they like reading better than they did before the summer session? We predict that they will.

We predicted that our students would improve more than students who did the regular summer program, and that they would like reading more than they did at the beginning of the summer.

The Students

The students for our study were drawn from elementary schools in one school district located in California. The district had a student population of approximately 34,000 and the majority of the students were minorities: 42% Hispanic, 21% Asian, 13% African American and 16% white. In addition, 35% of the district student population was classified as English language learners (ELL or Limited English Proficient) and 67% of the students received free or reduced lunch, that is, they were considered low income.

By way of comparison, for California as a whole, 26% of students are considered English learners, and 49% receive free or reduced lunch.[4] Our district, in other words, had somewhat more ELL children and a higher level of poverty. It is thus no surprise to learn that reading scores in general in this district were not high. Sixty-four percent of the students from this

Participants in our summer program were "struggling" readers. About 30% were considered "English learners."

school district scored below the proficient level on a standardized test of reading, the 1997 SAT/8 Reading test.

Students in this district were eligible for summer school because they were officially considered to be "struggling readers": They failed the sixth grade reading proficiency exam given by their district. A total of 360 sixth graders enrolled for the summer session. We placed 200 of them in the special Summer Reading Program (SRP), and 160, our "comparison group," were in the regular summer program. Thirty-one percent of the readers and 29% of the children in the comparison group were considered English learners.

Participation in the summer program was voluntary, but those who did poorly on the reading exam were strongly recommended to attend. There were, however, no negative consequences if students did not complete the entire six weeks of the program.

The Teachers

*Some of the
teachers were
unenthusiastic
about the
program at first.*

We gave all teachers questionnaires, probing their teaching experience, grades taught, and reasons for teaching summer school, among other things. There was no significant difference between the teachers of the reading group and the teachers of the comparison group.

Ten teachers taught in the Summer Reading Program. All were required to attend a one-day training session before the program began, presented by Fay Shin. The questionnaire results told us that only half of the teachers were there because they wanted to be, and it was clear during the training session that some of the teachers were not enthusiastic about the program. As we will see later, there was a phenomenal change in their attitudes soon after the program began.

During the six-week summer session, Fay met with the teachers once a week after class to discuss progress, to get teachers' reactions to the program, and to coach, that is, advise teachers what to do when problems occurred. Fay observed classes each day for the first two weeks and the last two weeks of the program, and discussed problems with teachers. The co-director and research assistants also made regular observations. In other words, we made sure that the teachers were really doing what they were supposed to be doing and that they understood the goals and nature of this program.

The Program

The summer program lasted for six weeks, and students were in school for four hours per day. The schedule for a typical day included the following:

1. 25 minutes of library time
2. 80 minutes of independent, recreational reading
3. 45 minutes of literature-based instruction
4. 45 minutes of project activity (e.g., book publishing, creation of a newspaper)
5. 25 minutes of read-aloud (teacher reads to the students), book sharing (pairs or groups), or other teacher-selected activities

We discuss each of these components in turn.

Library Time

We considered library time to be extremely important. We knew that the children in the program had little access to books outside of school, and needed to spend some time simply looking at books and browsing. Readers of this book think nothing of spending several hours in a bookstore, and emerging with one or two books. In fact, we regard this time as very well spent.

*Our first
priority was
making sure the
school library
had the best
collection
possible for
these children.*

*We made sure
the library was
well-stocked
with books from
the Goosebumps
series.*

Yet schoolchildren are often required to make a book selection from the school library in just a few minutes! Of course children were not required to browse; they were free to use the library time for recreational reading.

As we saw in Chapter 1, the better the school library, the higher the reading scores. With this in mind, we attempted to develop the best collection possible for these children, given our resources. We created the Summer Reading Program Library.

We had to do this. The school library was worse than dismal; it served a middle school of 1,200 students, and the supply of books was hopelessly inadequate. As we will see later, the most popular series of books for our students was the Goosebumps series. The school library had only six Goosebumps books, and only three books written by one of the best-known American authors of adolescent literature, Judy Blume.

We estimated that fewer than 10% of the books in the school library were right for these students. The rest were classics, old and outdated, and nonfiction. The library had no current magazines, and those that were available could not be checked out. We were told that they were kept behind the counter because they were always stolen or damaged by the students. The library did not have a credentialed school librarian and was staffed by a part-timer.

It was clear that the project had no chance of success unless children had more access to good books. Fay made sure the district director of curriculum was supplied with the current research on the importance of libraries, some of which we discussed in Chapter 1. In response to this, and to our requests, the allotment for the library was doubled. Each classroom was supplied with a collection of 400 books, and the central library was significantly strengthened. The district spent approximately $25 per student on popular paperback books and current magazines.

What They Read

A crucial characteristic of the program is that for the most part the students themselves selected what they wanted to read. Teachers suggested books, but their suggestions were based on their knowledge of the children's own interests and the teacher's knowledge of children's literature.

When we read for pleasure, we generally don't read anything unless it is of current interest to us right now. We rarely engage in delayed gratification, reading books that someday will be of benefit to us, books that will make us a better person. Struggling sixth graders should be allowed to read books that are interesting to them, for at least some of their reading. Moreover, as we have seen in Chapter 1, it appears to be the case that this kind of reading is the kind that contributes the most to language and literacy development.

We suspect, in fact, that "interest" is not enough, that for a text to really help in language and literacy development, it should be *compelling*, so interesting that the reader is "lost in the book," temporarily in another world. Csikszentmihalyi (1990) calls this "flow": In the state of flow, only the story exists and the sense of self is diminished and can even disappear. This is when real language acquisition and literacy development take place.[5]

The only way to guarantee that students are reading texts that are compelling for them, that will put them in a state of flow, is to allow them to select their own reading, with no requirement that children finish each book they start, even if the book was recommended by the teacher.

We felt that the best way to make sure students would enjoy the reading was to make sure that there were plenty of books available from R.L. Stine's very popular Goosebumps series. The series included the Goosebumps books themselves, considered appropri-

*Goosebumps is not
great literature,
but the stories
are often
compelling, and it
provides the
competence that
makes harder
reading possible.
Goosebumps also
increases
interest in
reading.*

ate for ages 9 to 12, books from the slightly more advanced Fear Street series, considered "young adult" reading, and books based on the Goosebumps TV episodes as well as books from another R.L. Stine series, Give Yourself Goosebumps.

We are the first to admit that Goosebumps is not great literature, and some people feel that encouraging this kind of reading material discourages the study of serious literature. We think the opposite is true. We recommend and encourage Goosebumps because we want children to be able to read great literature someday. Lighter reading provides the bridge that makes this possible. It helps children develop their vocabulary, their grammar, as well as get a feel for how stories are put together, or what experts call "the story grammar." In short, it helps make harder reading more comprehensible.

And Goosebumps isn't all that bad! We admire R.L. Stine for his ability to grab the reader's attention. We have read his books, and must admit that Stine makes you really want to know what will happen next. Here is an example. In the Fear Street novel *Welcome to Camp Nightmare,* a group of boys board a bus to go to summer camp. The driver is silent and grumpy. He drives them deeper and deeper into a forest, a forest that grows gloomier and gloomier as the day ends and the foliage gets thicker. When it is nearly dark, the driver abruptly stops, and tells the boys to get off the bus. As soon as they get off, the driver quickly drives away and the boys are left alone, deep in the dark and gloomy forest. End of chapter one! (If you want to know what happens, read the book.)

And of course we also admire R.L. Stine for what he has done to stimulate interest in reading and build reading competence for so many struggling readers.

We included, of course, more than R.L. Stine. Other series made available were the Sweet Valley series (Sweet Valley Kids, written at the second-grade level, Sweet Valley Twins, written at the fourth-grade level, and Sweet Valley High, aimed at junior high school and high school readers), The Baby-Sitters Club, Boxcar Children, and Animorphs.

The book collection also contained a variety of novels and children's picture books written by culturally diverse authors. The most popular of these authors included African American writers (Mildred Taylor, Julius Lester), Asian American authors (Laurence Yep, Yoshiko Uchida, Allen Say, Paul Yee), Native American authors (Joseph Bruchac, Rafe Martin and Michael Doris), and Hispanic American authors (Gary Soto, Alma Flor Ada, Sandra Cisneros, Arthur Dorros, Victor Villaseno).

Gary Soto's *Chato's Kitchen* was among the most widely read picture books, because of the humor, references to Mexican American food, and use of Spanish. Popular Southeast Asian books included *The Whispering Cloth—A Refugee's Story*, by Pegi Deitz Shea, and *The Lotus Seed* by Sherry Garland. The latter two were especially liked by Hmong and Southeast Asian students. It was rare for them to find books about their culture and that reflected their own experiences.

We also included nonfiction, books about animals, celebrities, and sports figures, which were very popular, as well as magazines, very high interest reading for children this age. Magazine titles included popular teen magazines such as *Teen, Young Miss, Seventeen, Sports Illustrated for Kids, Teen People, BMX, Hip Hop Connections, WWF, Car and Driver*, and over 40 other titles.

Our goal, of course, was not to convert our students to full-time readers of R.L. Stine and *Young Miss*. Our goal was to provide them with a desire to read and with the ability to read more. Research tells us that this is what happens—lighter reading serves as a conduit to heavier reading.[6]

The local newspaper donated 60 daily copies to the project and classroom sets of the newspaper were available for teachers to use with the entire class. In addition, classroom sets of SCOPE and READ Scholastic magazines were purchased.

We also included a wide variety of other books and magazines, and the local newspaper donated 60 copies of the daily paper.

Time for Recreational Reading

This was, of course, the core of the program. We realized that a full hour and 20 minutes a day for reading is a lot, so the reading time was divided into two 40-minute reading sessions.

Forty minutes of quiet reading time was provided twice a day.

During reading time students were allowed to select their own reading material and had the opportunity to read in class. The time was devoted to quiet reading: Students were not allowed to talk during recreational reading time (but see "book sharing" discussed later).

Conferencing

Teachers held brief conferences with each student each day and kept a log for each student.

Teachers held conferences with each student approximately once a day. The conferences were brief, lasting only about 10 minutes. The conferences included discussions of what students were reading, suggestions for additional reading, monitoring of student progress and comprehension, and some word attack skills. We present more details of what went on in these conferences in Appendix A.

Teachers kept a log for each student and made entries after each student-teacher conference. Included in the log was what students were reading and how much students appeared to be reading at home. This log was open-ended and required only the date of the student-teacher conference, and any additional notes the teacher wanted to write about what was discussed. Each student had a folder with the conference log in it that was kept at the teacher's desk.

We did not require book reports and students were not tested on what they read.

Instead of the dreaded book report[7] or test, students only had to fill out a simple book record. The book record sheet required only basic information: the book title, the author, a rating of 1 to 10 of the book, and a teacher's signature. Teachers signed the Book Record after asking one or more questions about the book. They might ask, for example, about a character in the book or the conclusion. (The teacher would generally glance at the student's book before asking about it, enough to get an idea of what the book was about and to begin asking some questions. Many students, however, were convinced that teachers had read every book!)

The teacher would sign off on the book record after she or he was satisfied that the student read the book. We employed, in other words, minimum accountability, only enough to ensure that the reading actually took place, being careful not to overdo it, not to require so much from the student that reading became a task rather than a pleasure. Examples of reading logs and book record sheets are in Appendix A.

Literature-Based Instruction

Class sets of popular literature were also used for literature instruction. Some of the novels used for this program were *Where the Red Fern Grows* by Wilson Rawls, *The Indian in the Cupboard* by Lynne Reid Banks, *Maniac Magee* by Jerry Spinelli, *The Giver* by Lois Lowry, *Hatchet* by Gary Paulsen, and *The Island of the Blue Dolphins* by Scott O'Dell.

In this part of the summer program, all students in a class read the same book (sometimes as homework, and sometimes class time was set aside for reading the book). The core of literature-based instruction was discussion of the novel, what the message of the book was, the students' opinion of the book, and how it related to the students' lives. The goal of literature, in our opinion, is twofold: It introduces students to fundamental philosophical ideas (Should we have a perfect, socially engineered society, as was attempted in the society described in *The Giver?*), and it introduces students to a wider range of books, which, we hope, will result in more self-selected reading.

Literature also included writing as well as discussion of the novel; writing is a powerful means of clarifying and stimulating thinking. Writing assignments were limited during the summer program,

No book reports were required. Instead, students kept a simple book record and discussed what they read with teachers during conferences.

The summer program also included some regular literature study in which all students read the same book, discussed it, and sometimes wrote about it.

however, as our goal was to build as much reading and vocabulary competence as possible. And we did not rely on the classic essay—instead teachers had students create graphic representations of stories, such as story maps, story boards, story cubes, time lines, webs and clusters, poetry writing, reflective journal writing, and character outlines.[8]

Project Activities

Projects included creating book posters, book markers, and book publishing. Teachers integrated their students' creative and artistic abilities with reading and writing.

"Project activities" included book writing and publishing, and making book markers. They typically entailed significant amounts of reading and writing.

Students participated eagerly in the projects. Many students interpreted this part of the day as "arts and crafts" time because it often involved drawing, coloring, and painting, and didn't realize they were actually participating in reading and writing activities. For example, when they were working on a book poster, the class first discussed how often we would see commercials or movie posters. Students were then asked to choose a favorite book and make a poster advertising it. They then wrote a short summary of the book and drew on their poster paper whatever they thought was appropriate.

Students also made book markers for themselves and their friends, which they decorated with stickers, drawings, or photos. Teachers laminated the markers at the end of the day.

Project time also included book writing. Some students wrote very short books, others wrote books with quite a bit of detail. The majority of the students wrote books about their lives (usually about themselves, families, or friends).

Teachers guided students through the composition process in writing their books. Students engaged in brainstorming and free writing, revising, and finally editing their manuscripts, and teachers put in a great deal of time editing and typing the final draft for the students. Finally, the students drew pictures on the typed pages and then either the teacher or students would bind the books.

The book publishing project was very successful and students were very proud of their final product, usually a spiral bound laminated book. One teacher brought in cotton patterned material she bought at a fabric store and bound thick cardboard with the fabric for the book covers.

These books were so authentic-looking that many students were in awe of how easy it was to make their own books.

Read-Alouds

There is no question that reading aloud to children (and to adults) is a very powerful means of stimulating the development of literacy.[9] Studies tell us that children who are read to a great deal, at home or at school, show better development of literacy than those read to less.[10] There are two reasons why read-alouds work: The first is obvious—they get children excited about books. Anyone who has ever worked in elementary school (or has even been to elementary school) knows this: The teacher reads *Charlotte's Web* to the students. The book soon disappears from the school library and the local bookstores. Children read *Charlotte's Web* again and again and sometimes memorize it. And then it is on to *Trumpet of the Swan, Stuart Little,* and eventually J.K. Rowling and Judy Blume. A second reason read-alouds work is that they provide exposure to the written language; they help children acquire the special grammar and vocabulary of stories, which makes actual reading much more comprehensible.

Read-alouds work because they encourage reading and because they provide exposure to the written language.

Our teachers read to the students every day. We knew it was working because teachers noticed that books were being checked out immediately after they read part of it to the class. California State University Dominguez Hills researcher Danny Brassell (2003) found the same thing occurred in his classroom. The title of his article is, in fact, "Sixteen books went home tonight: Fifteen were introduced by the teacher."

*Students were
more interested
in reading books
after the
teacher read
part in class.*

Read-alouds are excellent book advertisements, and led to students reading a wider variety of books, with reading interests spreading from fiction to nonfiction and biography.[11]

We also used reading aloud as part of the literature sessions, in order to motivate student interest. Many students, for example, were not initially interested in reading Lynne Reid Banks' *The Indian in the Cupboard* until the teacher read the chapter in which the Indian and the Cowboy come alive and meet for the first time. The teacher read the dialogue with such enthusiasm and drama (Texas accent and all) that her students were captivated. The class eagerly looked forward to hearing more of the book and reading it on their own, which led to lively class discussions.

Book Sharing

*Some time was
set aside for
students to
discuss their
reading with
each other.*

Book sharing was optional and happened two to three times a week. During this time, students were allowed to share and discuss their books in pairs, small groups, or as a whole class. Participation was completely voluntary, that is, students were not required to share. Many, however, did. They clearly enjoyed talking about what they read with a friend. If students did not want to do book sharing, they could read on their own. On average, about half of the students chose to read independently during book sharing time.

In other words, students had a choice of reading or talking. As mentioned earlier, students were not allowed to talk during the regular recreational reading time: "Sustained silent reading" was really silent. This means that if a student wanted to discuss a book, she had to wait for book sharing time. This was, in our opinion, a good way to solve the problem that comes up frequently when sustained silent reading is done: Should reading be completely silent or should students be given the chance to discuss their reading? The answer is "yes" to both options, by providing a separate quiet reading time and a time during which discussion is permitted (but not required).

Recall that 160 children were in the "comparison group." Six teachers worked with these children. We did not give these teachers any specific curriculum to follow during the summer. The comparison teachers provided us with their daily lesson plans, and our assistants observed several of their classes.

Four out of the six comparison group teachers said they included sustained silent reading, but the sessions lasted for only 20 minutes per day, far less than the amount of reading done by the reading group.

The teachers told us that they taught their classes with materials they used during the school year, with an emphasis on skills (e.g., grammar, spelling, and vocabulary) and workbooks. The average comparison group teacher spent about half the class time (almost two hours per day) on skills. One teacher, for example, told us that she did 50 minutes of vocabulary work, 50 minutes of grammar study, one hour of literature (which meant guided reading and discussion), and 20 minutes of sustained silent reading.

In other words, the comparison group was a real comparison group, with children getting the curriculum children typically get in schools throughout the United States during the academic year.

The Tests

As we will see later, the reaction of students and teachers to the reading program was excellent. The district curriculum director appreciated this enthusiasm, but made it clear to us that the district would not consider continuing the program without results from standardized tests. The voices of the teachers and student opinion did not count—to justify the program to the school board, test scores are what counted.

Like many others in our profession, we are not in agreement with the testing hysteria that has gripped

*Our study was
evaluated with
the use of
standardized
tests.*

schools. We are not opposed to assessment, but we are opposed to excessive and inappropriate testing, testing that fills the school day with test preparation, and that encourages mindless drill as preparation. We were confident, however, that our students would do well on any kind of test, that their reading would result in a natural acquisition or absorption of the "skills" they needed to pass the tests.

We made sure that at least some of the tests that were used were "standardized tests," that is, tests constructed by private companies and research organizations. An advantage to using standardized tests is that testing experts have already determined, from extensive calculations, that the tests are reliable and valid. A reliable test is a dependable test, that is, if we give the test again to the same people, it will give similar results. A valid test means that the test measures what it is supposed to measure. In the case of standardized reading tests, it means that the test scores agree fairly well with the results of other tests. This is not a completely satisfying way of determining validity, but it is helpful. If our students do well on these tests, they would do well on other tests that society accepts as measures of reading ability.

Our students took two standardized reading tests both before and after the summer session, with pre and post-testing done five and one-half weeks apart. One was the *ALTOS Reading Achievement Test*, developed by Northwest Evaluation Association and administered by the school district. The ALTOS has several sections, covering reading, "language usage" (grammar and punctuation), and spelling. We added a second standardized test, the *Nelson-Denny Reading Comprehension Test*, designed for students in grades 3 through 9, developed by the Houghton Mifflin Company. The Nelson-Denny includes reading and vocabulary and is available in two different forms, which are considered equivalent. One was given at the beginning of the session and one at the end.

The Testing Results:
Some Preliminaries

Before giving the test scores, we need to discuss attrition and engagement.

As we noted earlier, summer school is voluntary in the district we studied, and we can expect that not all students will do the entire program. Of course, students drop out for a variety of reasons that have nothing to do with academics. Fay interviewed some of the students who said they were leaving the program. Reasons included a family vacation, babysitting obligations, excessive absences (the summer school absence policy was very strict), and getting into a fight, which results in immediate expulsion.

If, however, students drop out of one program more than another, this could mean that one program was more popular. But attrition rates were nearly identical for the reading and the comparison programs: At the beginning of the summer, both groups had an average of 20 students per class. By the end of the summer, the reading classes averaged 14.3 students (a total of 81 students) and the comparison classes averaged 13.2 students (a total of 52 students). This rate of attrition is typical for summer sessions in this district.

Teacher observations revealed that at the beginning of the session, about 30% to 40% of the students were not really involved in reading, but were pretending to read or were otherwise occupied. By the end of the first week, however, it was clear that nearly all students were engaged in real reading. Some of the disengagement at the start of the session was the result of choosing books that were too difficult; this problem gradually disappeared thanks to teacher help in book selection during the conferences.

We present the test scores only for those students who took the standardized tests at the beginning and the end of the summer. Thus, our entire group was not tested, but we still tested a considerable number of children, more than enough to give us confidence that our results are valid indicators of student growth.

Approximately the same percentage of students completed the summer program in both the reading group and the comparison group.

Nearly all students were engaged in reading by the end of the first week.

The Pretest Results

Even though the children in the reading group and the comparison group were from similar backgrounds, and there was no effort made to put the better readers in one of the groups, just to be sure we gave all children pretests. It was a good thing we did this: Those in the reading group scored a bit lower than those in the comparison group. On the Nelson-Denny reading comprehension test, for example, the children in the reading group scored at the fourth grade level, but those in the comparison group scored at level 5.4 (fifth grade, four months), nearly a year and a half difference. The difference was much less on the Nelson-Denny vocabulary test (the reading group scored 5.3, the comparisons scored 5.4).

We used a statistical technique that allowed us to pretend this pretest difference did not exist, that is, it was adjusted for the pretest scores and produced an adjusted posttest score, a score that students would have gotten if the pretest scores had indeed been the same. This valuable statistical tool is called analysis of covariance.

Gains in reading comprehension were excellent: Readers gained over a year on one test, and five months on another, after only five and a half weeks of reading. Comparisons made only two months gain on one test and made no gains on the other.

The Posttest Results

The ALTOS Test

The typical district scores for grades 3 through 8 show an average growth of four points from fall to spring for the reading tests. During the five and a half weeks, the reading group gained an equivalent of 2.2 points, which is approximately five months. There was no growth in the comparison group.

The Nelson-Denny Reading Comprehension Test

Those in the comparison group made modest gains on this test, improving from the 5.4 level on the average to the 5.6 level, about a two-month gain. The readers, however, made astounding gains on this test, moving from an average score of 4.0 to 5.3, a gain of one year and three months.

The results of the Nelson-Denny vocabulary test were less spectacular but still quite acceptable, with both groups growing six months (the comparison group improved from level 5.4 to 6.0, and the readers improved from 5.3 to 5.9).

Thus, after only five and a half weeks of reading, students improved five months on a general test of reading (the ALTOS), six months on vocabulary on another test (Nelson-Denny vocabulary test), and over a year on a test of reading comprehension (Nelson-Denny reading comprehension test). These are impressive results.

Before we rejoice, however, we must ask some hard questions: Will the gains continue after the program ends? Will these children continue to read? Did we convert reluctant readers into enthusiastic readers? Will we have to supply these students with the same program each summer? We look now at what the teachers said and what the children themselves said.

The readers and the comparisons made the same gains on a test of vocabulary, improving about six months after five and a half weeks.

What the Teachers Said

All 10 of the teachers who taught the reading group felt strongly about the success of the program. They told us that they noticed an obvious and striking difference in the students' attitudes toward reading.

A main reason for the improvement, they said, is that so many popular books and magazines were available, and the reading material was genuinely interesting. The students were actually excited about reading and about being able to take the books and magazines home. Eve Marin confirmed the importance of access:

> Silent reading was always done in my classroom for 10 minutes a day but the biggest problem was getting the books into the students' hands. The library was rarely open when the students needed to go. However, during this summer

Teachers felt the program worked well. One reason was access to interesting reading.

*Our results
confirm that
contrary to
popular opinion,
children really
do like to read—
but they need
access to the
right books.*

program I saw my students continually reading their novels. They had complete access to the books that they wanted and once they knew the parts of the newspaper and knew they were going to receive the newspaper every day they looked forward to their daily reading of the newspaper on their own. (Marin, paper submitted at end of program)

This reaction is reassuring; it confirms what research says and what few people appear to know: Children (and teenagers) really do like to read—but they need to have access to genuinely interesting reading material.

There have been concerns that if we let children read whatever they want to read they will stick to very easy books and not progress to more challenging material. There has been no recent research on this topic. Studies show that children gradually expand their reading tastes, but this research is over 50 years old. Our teachers confirmed that children gradually choose more challenging reading material, even over the short span of six weeks. Some students, for example, began with Goosebumps, but eventually moved on to Fear Street.

*Teachers also
attributed
improvement to
the daily
conferences with
individual
students.*

The Conferences

The teachers felt the daily reading logs and monitoring were very important to the success of the program. At the beginning of the program, the conferencing time between the student and teacher turned out to be the most challenging part, yet, it eventually turned out to be the most rewarding part of the program.

Teachers used the conferences to focus on each student's particular reading level and needs. Students appreciated this individual attention. Teachers felt that the one-on-one time was essential to monitor and encourage student progress. There was a noticeable difference in the students once the teachers started to monitor and keep track of their daily reading. (We will tell you more about this in Chapter 3.)

Students' Reactions: Interviews

We interviewed the students at the beginning and end of the six-week session.

Results from the student interviews revealed that 86% of the students said they read more at home since the program started. They also stated they liked reading better and that they will continue to read after the program ends. In fact, over 80% of the students recommended that the program be continued. This reaction corresponds to what the teachers told us and is very reassuring. If students like reading better, and say they will continue to read, this means that we have succeeded.

As we saw earlier, our test score results were very good. But we consider these results more important— our real goal was not only short-term gains, as welcome as they are. Our goal was long-term enthusiasm for reading, a guarantee of adequate literacy development.

We need to emphasize, however, that this guarantee only holds if children have access to the right reading material, which is not usually the case for children of poverty.

When we asked why they were enthusiastic about the program, the students told us the same thing the teachers did: It was because so much good reading material was available and they were allowed to choose their own reading. And they also told us something the teachers did not: The children liked the program because of their teachers. When asked for clarification for responding "the teachers" they all stated that the daily conferencing (one-on-one) and encouragement was a major motivating factor, a topic we return to in Chapter 3.

Nine students read over 40 books each; that's more than one book a day. Many of the students (65%) claimed that they were not used to reading so

Students reported reading more at home after the summer program, and said they will continue to read more. Most felt the program should be continued.

Students agreed with the teachers: The program worked because good books were available, and because of the conferencing with teachers. Students also said they appreciated being able to select their own reading.

much at school and home, and one student said, "I never read so much in my entire life!"

We asked the students which parts of the school day they liked the best. The clear winner was the independent reading time. When asked if they would like to continue to have time for recreational reading during the regular school year, 76% stated yes, 23% stated no, and 1% responded that they didn't know.

Students' Reactions: Written

Students were asked to write an anonymous evaluation of the summer school reading program on the last day of class. We have included a few of their comments here. The majority of the comments were positive. Out of 104 written evaluations, only 6 had negative comments.

*The most popular
author was
R.L. Stine.*

Here are some of their comments. We present them as the students wrote them, unedited and uncorrected (remember that about 30% of the students were English learners).

Without question, the most frequently mentioned author was R.L. Stine, which agrees with what other readers say, and of course we made sure plenty of Goosebumps books were available:

- *This summer school has got me more in to reading than I ever imangin. I start likeing R. l Stine, Goosebumps, and bady Sitter's club. I even start reading the newspaper. I know now how fun reading is.*
- *The summers school pogram was very cool. In my raeding class I loved It becuase I got to read more. When we wen't to the libery I started to read more Goosebumps and know I am reading more.*
- *I like to lei down and read and I Thiank that I will read more at home I like to read R.L. Stine he is a good writer.*
- *I Like all of the Goosebumps Book's.*
- *This summer school reading program is great. It has improved my reading alot. The best part of this pro-*

gram is the there were a lot of Goose-Bumps to read. Now, it has made me like reading more.

- *I Like the's Reding Protran I lend to Rend Bander [read better]. I hop you have it nak yer [next year] I Like all of the Goesbums Book's.*

Students confirmed that they appreciated being able to select their own reading:

- *This is what I like about summer school is because you. Get to read books when you have free time and you get. To pick your very on book you wont to read. In your teacher can help you when you wont help. thats what I like. Thank you*

Most students told us that they liked the free reading sessions the best, but some preferred library time and read-aloud time. The least popular appeared to be the literature sessions:

- *This yare in summer school, I thouht the best part was when we went outside and read. I liked it because we got to cool of and have fun at the same time. I liked my teacher as well she is a great teacher, and I think you should keep her next year. Thank you*
- *I think the class is good becuse I llike to read more because I could learn how to read. What I did not like in class is to do* [literature-based instruction] *because I do not lik do work. I like to read more. I like to go to the library because I like to read at the library.*
- *I think that the best thing I liked about summer school is silent reading. It was fun to read silently. Even though I have not read a lot of books I still did my best. I did like the books I have read and I had a lot of fun in summer school. So peace out Muir* [Muir is the pseudonym for the name of the school].
- *What I liked about this class was reading aloud and library becuase it is fun and good for me too.*

Some hoped that regular school would include free reading and some wanted to do the program again next summer:

- *It helps me on reading. When I go to my regular school I want it like this because It helps me more. I might attend summer school next year. I thought it was hard, but when I came it was interesting. I think it helps me. I like this class.*

- *I think that we had good books to read. I think they should have this program every summer. This progam has done me a lot of good. I would want to comeback if they are going to have this program agine.*

- *I relely like the 30 min. reding. It shod be in evrey classroom. I hope. I will remeber all of it. I relely like the librery. It shod be every city. I think liberys are good.*

Some confirmed that their interest in reading grew over the course of the session—we regard this as the single most important result of the study:

- *Summer school was great I had fun. The things I liked about summer school was Reading the books and stuff. Well at first I didn't like to Read like fear street ones. Maybe I will even Read at home to. May be I'll come back next year.*

- *Summer School program was fun. I enjoy reading now. Then I didn't like to read. We read and play games it was fun. We listen to miusc and get book from the Lirbery.*

- *I think this program is great now I'm not so lazy any more like I used to be. Now I read all the tine this program help me and others a hole lot.*

- *I think I learn much n the progran. My mom said you read batter then I was reading before. My mom proud of me.*

- *I feel wonderful about this program. When I first started reading I hated it but then I got really into it when the teachers at the library helped me alot at reading.*

- *I like the program because I really improve. Now I start reading book because of this program and most the book in the library good but mostly I only read horror book and I like it now will read most book.*

Our most important result: Student interest in reading increased.

But there were exceptions:

- *I read more books than ever before. I think I read better I still don't like reading much though.*

Some students had some constructive criticism:

- *What I didn't like is the novel Home Swet Home, Good-bye. Why? because it was broing. What I like is reading my own book because it help me in my reading alot.*
- *What was okay was the teachs you how to read and the free read and the books in the libery. What I want to change is that free read three time a day. and change it all for next year.*
- *In the summer reading program, silent reading was the best because it can be piece and quiet so you can read. They should put in alot more books about the Simpsons and about sports in for the next year.*

And as we noted, there were a few negative comments:

- *I did not like the program because it was boring. It was boring because most of the time we were reading. But if I had to pick what was the best it would be when the teacher read to us. I liked it because you just sit and lison.*
- *I don't like the school reading program because you have to do to much reading on class*

While most students who liked the program found the books interesting, at least one student appeared to be motivated more by an extrinsic factor, reading the most books. This was, however, rare:

- *I think this summer school program was okay because of the reading. They made me read alot and after a while I had the most books read in my class. I think I'll come back next year.*

And we received some global praise:

- *I think that this program has been a great infulense on my and my read skills. Everyboby else in my class room feel the same.*[12]

Book Circulation

Table 2.1 shows the daily amount of books and magazines checked out from the library. Note that the students also had books available to them in their classroom library—these checkouts were not included. There are several very interesting trends in this table.

First, the number of books taken out per day, per student increases. Recall that the number of students in the reading program decreased over the summer! We began the summer with 200 children in the reading group. That means that students were taking out one book for every eight students the first week. But by the end, we had 120 students. This means that by the end of the summer, they were taking out about one book each day for every two students, a fourfold increase in the number of books checked out. And again, this figure is based only on the school library—books were also available in the classroom.

Notice also that book circulation increased over the summer while magazine circulation tended to decrease, which suggests to us that students were indeed selecting more challenging material as the program progressed.

The overwhelming majority (80%) of the books checked out were Goosebumps. Other very popular books were *Men in Black* and *Batman and Robin* (based on current movies), and *Calvin and Hobbes.* We stocked about a dozen of *Men in Black* and *Batman and Robin* and eight copies of *Calvin and Hobbes* (they were expensive), but it seemed as if they were always checked out and there were waiting lists of students wanting to read them. Also popular were sports books and

Table 2.1

Library Daily Log

		Books	Magazines
Week 1	Monday	24	71
	Tuesday	27	93
	Wednesday	n.a.	73
	Thursday	68	64
	Friday	103	53
Week 2	Monday	109	69
	Tuesday	84	54
	Wednesday	91	37
	Thursday	91	46
	Friday	88	34
Week 3	Monday	96	41
	Tuesday	85	33
	Wednesday	88	38
	Thursday	88	22
	Friday (no school)		
Week 4	Monday	77	24
	Tuesday	88	25
	Wednesday	67	30
	Thursday	80	26
	Friday	70	31
Week 5	Monday	105	20
	Tuesday	66	19
	Wednesday	n.a.	25
	Thursday	92	23
	Friday	75	20
Week 6	Monday	73	38
	Tuesday	49	30

n.a. = data not available

Note: Students also had books available for checkout in their own classrooms. Number of books checked out from classrooms were not recorded.

*Students tended
to select books
that were at
their grade
level, that were
right for them.*

*Students from
the comparison
group and ESL
class also used
the library, and
library visits
increased during
the course of the
program.*

biographies of athletes (e.g., Michael Jordan, Barry Bonds).

Most of the books the students selected were written at the third and fourth grade level. In other words, students selected books that were, in general, right for them: Recall that the average reading level for our readers at the beginning of the summer was exactly 4.0, the beginning of grade 4, as measured by the Nelson-Denny reading comprehension test.[13]

The Spill-Over

Of course, the reading students were not the only ones allowed to use the library. During the second week of the program, other students used it, students from the comparison group and students in a special program for English language learners. They were allowed to visit the library in the morning before school started and during recess.

As more students heard about the books, daily visits to the library increased. The average number of students visiting the library before school began in the morning was 21. The daily average number of students during the recess break was 24. There were a few days where the number was as high as 38! Because the Goosebumps Summer students already had daily access to the library, the majority (90%) of the students coming in during recess were from either the control group or the English Language Development (ELD) classes in a separate program at the same school site.

Our volunteer librarian Winnie Llamera told us about ESL students' enthusiasm for magazines in a report she wrote:

A notable change was that a sizable number (more than 20) of nonreading program students were in the library at 7:30 a.m. before classes started. A majority of them were Asians who showed a preference for magazines. A handful of females were interested in the young women's magazines and were flipping the pages while chattering in their native language. Several of the persistent ones begged to be given the chance to borrow books and magazines. Three students were then referred to Kathy Marshall (the coordinator).

Clearly the library was providing something these students could not easily find elsewhere.

Interviews with the Top Readers

We were very interested in getting more details about eight special students. Before the summer program began, these students were clearly reluctant readers— they told us that before the summer program they rarely read on their own. But during the summer, each of these eight students read over 40 books, nearly one book a day. We wanted to know why.

The answer was simple but profound. They read so much, they told us, because the books were "fun and interesting," and teachers encouraged them to read. They did not read for rewards or recognition. Their motivation was intrinsic, not extrinsic. And most of the books they read were from the Goosebumps series.

Earlier, in Chapter 1, we presented studies that suggested strongly that children who are "reluctant readers" are in general only reluctant because they have little or no access to interesting reading. Our interviews confirmed this.

One of the eight students, Brian, commented that he had never seen so many books that were fun to read and that he was happy that he could take them home. During the interview, Brian stated, "In school the books are boring, and at home we don't have books. My teacher let me take home books and she kept telling me to read at home."

All of the students commented on how easy it was to get books that they liked. They all said that they

Interviews with once-reluctant readers who become enthusiastic readers confirmed the importance of access and conferences with teachers.

never really had the opportunity or desire to have a lot of books. They used to think reading was boring, but because this program offered many interesting and fun books, it changed their attitude about reading.

Another student commented that the only reason why he read so many books was because the teacher "told him to." When I asked him what he meant, he just kept saying that because the teacher asked him every day what he read, he felt that he "had to read" at home. But then, later, he said he just liked to read, and "anyway, there was nothing else to do at home during the summer." We return to this perceptive comment in the next chapter, when we go a little deeper into the widely discussed issue of how we encourage children to read, beyond simply supplying books.

A Quick Summary

The results of the testing, observations, interviews, surveys, weekly teacher evaluations and discussions were positive and all said the same thing, which is very reassuring (researchers call this "reliability").

- The test results were excellent, with the readers doing at least as well as comparison students on one measure, and doing spectacularly better on two. This is in agreement with the research literature on sustained silent reading and other in-school reading methods in which children are allowed to select their own reading, research that we discussed in chapter one. As impressive and important as these short-term results are, we were much more concerned with students' reactions to the program and whether they liked reading more at the end of summer than they did at the beginning—our goal is long-term improvement.

- The teachers told us that the program had a tremendous impact on the students. They acknowledged that the program would not have been successful if it were not for the books and magazines available, the one-on-one monitoring, and the support staff. Four of the 10 teachers reported that they had implemented independent reading time in their regular classroom during the school year before this pilot program, but with very little success. They attributed the difference to the access to the magazines and Goosebumps books and the one-on-one conferencing.

- The data collected from the interviews and surveys shows a phenomenal change in the students' attitude toward reading. Students said they were now reading more on their own. They also attributed the change to access to "fun and interesting" reading material, and were especially enthusiastic about Goosebumps.

*N*OTES

1. Stephen Krashen published an exhaustive review of the most popular incentive system used in reading, Accelerated Reader (AR). AR consists of four components: providing interesting books, providing time to read (one hour per day), quizzes on the content of the books (with an emphasis on facts), and rewards for points earned on the quizzes. As we saw in Chapter 1, there is strong evidence that the first two components are effective: Children who have access to interesting reading material and a time and place to read will read more and make more progress in literacy development. There is no direct evidence that tests the efficacy of the third and fourth components. No study has been done to see how AR compares to a program containing only the first two components, access to books and time to read. One must conclude that AR has never really been properly evaluated, despite a plethora of studies. Stephen Krashen, The (lack of) experimental evidence supporting the use of accelerated reader. *Journal of Children's Literature* 29(2)(2003), 9, 16–30. See also: Stephen Krashen, Accelerated reader: Evidence still lacking. *Knowledge Quest* 33(3)(2005), 48–49.

In addition to the lack of experimental evidence justifying this practice, there is the danger that rewarding an activity that is already pleasurable sends the message that the activity is not really pleasant, and can extinguish interest in the activity. There is some experimental evidence confirming that this is true for reading; see Vonnie McLoyd, The effects of extrinsic rewards of differential value on high and low intrinsic interest. *Child Development* 10(1979), 1010–19. For a complete discussion of the drawbacks of incentives, see Alfie Kohn's book, *Punished by Rewards* (Houghton Mifflin, 1999).

Nevertheless, incentives remain popular in summer reading programs. Here are just a few examples. In a program in Pinellas, Florida, for each ten minutes the students read continuously, they get a yellow sticky note, which can be exchanged eventually for "treats" (Ron Matus, How do you teach a child to read? *St. Petersburg Times,* July 7, 2004). The public library in Canby, Oregon, asks summer readers to "sign a contract to read for 10 hours during the summer to earn a free book and the chance to enter drawings for other prizes" (www.ci.canby.or.us/ Canbylibrary/library.htm). The Bucyrus Public Library in Ohio announced: "Read 3 books get a Subway coupon, read 5 books get a Little Caesars' coupon and read 10 books get a $1.00 coupon for Capitol 5 Cinemas! Enter for special prize drawings by reading and reviewing books and attending programs. Drawings are held following the programs!" (www.bucyrus.lib.oh.us/yasrc04.htm).

2. For examples of summer reading programs focusing on skills, see Schacter (1999). The children in Schacter's study were high poverty first graders who had two hours per day of reading over eight weeks, with a focus on phonics, oral reading, and "comprehension skills." The summer reading group did much better than a comparison group on a number of tests of reading. This result, however, does not show that a skills focus is effective. First, the reading group was read to daily, a practice known to be effective in increasing literacy. Second, they engaged in some actual reading, from a basal, and in sessions with tutors. Third, it appears to be the case that the comparison group had no special program. In other

words, they did nothing. Being children of poverty, it is likely that they had little or no access to reading material, a suspicion consistent with the finding that their reading scores declined over the summer. John Schacter, *Reducing Social Inequality in Elementary School Reading Achievement: Establishing Summer Literacy Camps for Disadvantaged Children* (Santa Monica, CA: Milken Family Foundation, 2003). Finally, Elaine Garan (2000) has shown that a heavy emphasis on phonics clearly impacts tests given at grade 1, but has no significant impact on tests of reading comprehension given after grade 1. Schacter's study, thus, is not counterevidence to our claim that recreational reading is the crucial element in developing literacy over the summer, and at other times as well. Elain Garan, *Resisting Reading Mandates* (Portsmouth, NH: Heinemann, 2000).

3. The "proper" way to state a hypothesis is to predict no difference between the groups, that is, to state the hypothesis as a "null" hypothesis, for example, "There will be no difference between the readers and those in the comparison group." We have chosen to use ordinary language to state our hypotheses here, predicting that the summer readers will do better.

4. For statistics on California, see www.ed-data.k12.ca.us.

5. Mihalyi Csikszentmihalyi, *Flow: The Psychology of Optimal Experience* (New York: Harper Perennial, 1990).

6. LaBrant, in 1958, documented the fact that readers' tastes generally broaden as they get older. Lou LaBrant, An evaluation of free reading. In *Research in the Three R's*, ed. C. Hunnicutt and W. Iverson (New York: Harper and Brothers, 1958), pp. 154–61.

For evidence that light reading serves as a conduit to heavy reading, see the case histories of comic book readers collected in Krashen's *The Power of Reading* (2004). These dedicated and sophisticated adult readers regarded comic books as an important stepping stone in their literacy development.

Carlsen and Sherrill (1988) analyzed "reading biographies" written by university students who were mostly librarians, English teachers, or training to become one or the other. Carlsen and Sherrill tell us that "those who had access to old boxes of series books indulged themselves to the point of satiation and then moved on to other types of books" (p. 149).

Carlsen and Sherriff make this astute observation: "Although the writers of the autobiographies ultimately selected professions for themselves where books were valued (English teachers and librarians), the writers were not 'childhood wonders' who read adult classics in second grade. They tasted and read the usual fare of children's classics and then moved through the series books to the books on subjects that had predictable appeal for youngsters" (p. 150). In other words, The Summer Reading Program attempted to facilitate a natural progression of reading interests.

In addition, Carlsen and Sherriff's students tell us the danger of the premature introduction of "classic literature": "Some writers revealed that they were absolutely baffled by the classics . . . some respondents withdrew completely from the world of books because the classics were so far beyond their ability" (p. 154). The Summer Reading Program is an attempt to make sure this doesn't happen, by helping children build competence in literacy that will make more "serious" reading much more comprehensible. G. Robert Carlsen and Anne Sherrill, *Voices of Readers* (Urbana, IL: NCTE, 1988).

7. Carlsen and Sherrill (1988) reported that "book reports were almost universally disliked by the respondents. Book reports did more to kill the young people's interest in reading than to promote it" (p. 154). Occasionally book reports had a positive effect, "but for most of the respondents, book reports became a source of irritation, ranging from mild to violent dislike on the part of the writers . . . young people [resorted] to all kinds of subterfuges when faced with doing the mandatory book report" (p. 155). Here is an example. One student wrote: "I can remember giving an oral book report on *The Old Man and the Sea* which was a great success, so I proceeded to give the same report for the next two years" (p. 103). Another student found a different solution: "Sometimes in school I had to start writing book reports. They were terrible, but I learned that *Classic Comics* were a big help" (p. 102).

One respondent summarized the reasons for this reaction: "the writing of the book report inevitably followed the reading of the book. Invariably the reports had to include a biographical sketch of the author, the period, the setting, the listing of the major and minor characters, a summary of the plot, and finally . . . what I learned or got from the book. Bewilderment led to resentment. I wasn't reading anything for sheer entertainment as I once had" (p. 99).

8. See, for example, Carole Cox, *Teaching Language Arts: A Student and Response Centered Classroom* (Upper Saddle River, NJ: Pearson, 2005); G. Tompkins, *Literacy for the 21st Century: Teaching Reading and Writing in Grades 4 through 8* (Upper Saddle River, NJ: Pearson, 2004); Regie Routman, *Invitations: Changing as Teachers and Learners K–12* (Portsmouth, NH: Heinemann, 1994).

9. Surveys show that a substantial percentage of parents read aloud to their children regularly. Jim Trelease's superb book, *The Read-Aloud Handbook* (New York: Penguin, 2001, 5th ed.) deserves much of the credit for popularizing read-alouds in North America. We also recommend his website, www.trelease-on-reading.com, which includes his speaking schedule; his talks are as captivating as his book.

10. Adriana Bus, Marinus Van Ijzendoorn, and Anthony Pellegrini, Joint book reading makes for success in learning to read: A meta-analysis on intergenerational transmission of literacy. *Review of Educational Research* 65(1995), 1–21; Henk Blok, Reading to young children in educational settings: A meta-analysis of recent research. *Language Learning* 49(2)(1999), 343–71.

11. Danny Brassell, Sixteen books went home tonight: Fifteen were introduced by the teacher. *The California Reader* 36(3)(2003), 33–39. For another study with similar results, see Miriam Martinez, Nancy Roser, Jo Worthy, Susan Strecker, and Philip Gough, Classroom libraries and children's book selections: Redefining "access" in self-selected reading. In *Inquires in Literacy: Theory and Practice. Forty-sixth Yearbook of The National Reading Conference,* ed. Charles Kinzer, Kathleen Hinchman, and Donald Leu (Chicago: National Reading Conference, 1997), pp. 265–72.

12. One of the teachers asked her students to fill out a short survey on the last day of class. Students were

asked not to put their names on the survey. Here are the questions she asked her students and their responses:

- I like reading better now than I did six weeks ago. Yes 10/No 2
- I will continue to read books for pleasure. Yes 10/No 2
- I liked having the teacher read out loud to me every day Yes 3/No 9

The students clearly liked the reading class; they felt that they had improved and liked reading better. They were not, however, enthusiastic about being read to. This is surprising because the read-alouds seemed to be working: Students tended to take home books that were read to them and some students indicated that they liked them, and several indicated that the read-aloud time was their favorite part of the day. These particular students may not have liked how read-alouds were done in their class. Regardless, this negative response gives us some faith that their responses to the first two questions were honest: These students were not trying to please the teacher with their answers.

13. Other studies have shown that when students are allowed to select their own reading, they do not stick to very easy books: They typically choose books that are about at their reading level and even above it. Vera Southgate, Helen Arnold, and Sandra Johnson, *Extending Beginning Reading* (London: Heinemann Educational Books, 1981); Beverly Boulware and Christy Foley, Recreational reading: Choices of fourth graders. *Journal of Reading Education* 23(2)(1998), 17–22.

ALTOS Test Results

	n	Pretest	Posttest	Adjusted Mean
Experimental	116	195.3 (11.5)	197.5 (11.9)	198.9
Comparison	58	200.7 (10.4)	199.3 (11.2)	196.25

Standard deviations in parentheses.

Nelson-Denny: Comprehension

	n	Pretest	Posttest	Gain
Experimental	81	4 (1.5)	5.3 (2.1)	1.3
Comparison	52	5.4 (2.2)	5.6 (2.2)	0.2

Standard deviations in parentheses.

Nelson-Denny: Vocabulary

	n	Pretest	Posttest	Gain
Experimental	81	5.3 (1.9)	5.9 (1.9)	0.6
Comparison	47	5.4 (1.8)	6.0 (2.0)	0.6

Nelson-Denny mean scores represent grade equivalent scores, not raw scores.

Standard deviations in parentheses.

CHAPTER 3

What We Learned

Enthusiastic readers say that librarians and teachers encouraged them to read and recommended specific books.

The Summer Reading Program taught us a lot. It confirmed some of the ideas we already had, but also forced us to change our thinking in some ways. The experience confirmed our view that when they are given interesting, comprehensible books, most children will actually read them and will enjoy them. And it confirmed our view that reading is beneficial for language and literacy development.

The most important lesson we learned was that we underestimated what it took to get children reading. Access to good books, while necessary, was not sufficient. We needed to give at least some children some real encouragement. Our experiences gave us a good start in understanding just what kind and how much encouragement was effective.

There has been only limited discussion in the professional literature on whether we should actively encourage or even push children to read, and recommend certain books. It has clearly helped in some cases. Here are a few of the reading autobiographies of education students in the fields of library science and English language arts from *Voices of Readers*, by G. Robert Carlsen and Anne Sherrill.[1]

(1) I also began to read more frequently when I took a course in twelfth grade called Individualized Reading . . . At the time I liked politics and read stories about negative utopias . . . My teacher thought I was getting too bogged down with political books and so recommended J.D. Salinger and William Golding. I feel this course introduced me to literature and influenced me toward majoring in English. (p. 98)

(2) In high school with the exception of one teacher, we had an almost entirely free reading program . . . my teachers let me choose my own books with an occasional suggestion. I usually tried the books they suggested and found most of them fascinating reading. (p. 99)

(3) . . . a librarian by the name of Miss R. probably guided my reading more than anyone. However, she did it so skillfully that I have just now come to realize it. I spent a lot of time in the public library and Miss R. always had a reading suggestion. It sometimes surprised me that the books she suggested were quite good. This is probably how I came to read most of the good books as well as my own selections. I was a prolific reader. (p. 113)

(4) After I had made several trips to the library, Miss B. became aware of the interest in horses that had grown in me and recommended book after book on horses for me to read. I went through all of Walter Farley's books as well as every other book on horses that the library owned. (p. 113)

(4) About this time I discovered the public library. Here I spent two hours every afternoon. I remember with awe and affection the plump librarian who never shushed, never frowned, who led me constantly to new books. One day she asked me if I know about gods and goddesses and showed me to the mythology section. I scarcely moved for a month. (p. 114)

The literature also provides us with cases in which encouragement didn't work. *Voices of Readers* provides us with this one:

(5) The librarian . . . always tried to interest my friend and me in books that had won Newbury prizes or books of exceptional quality for our age bracket. At the time (grade school) I was more interested in horses, so I generally resisted his efforts . . . There was one book I took home once to get him off my back. I would still pass up *The Last of the Mohicans* today, because of the extreme pressure I experienced as a youth to read it. (p. 115)

Sometimes direct encouragement doesn't work.

Encouraging didn't work in Vincent Greaney and Mary Hegarty's study, published in 1987: Parents of less-adept fifth grade readers were *more* likely to encourage the children to read the newspaper than the parents of better readers.[2]

Tanesha

The breakthrough for us was Fay's experience with Tanesha, a sixth grader in the program who read at the fourth grade level. Fay became interested in Tanesha's progress because of a particular incident that happened during conferencing time.

One Friday, when Tanesha was in the library, I pulled her folder and conference log, and asked her to read to me. She read one page from the Goosebumps book she was reading. She read it without difficulty and with a high level of accuracy. I asked her a few questions and it was obvious that she had understood what she had read.

When she finished reading the next page, I asked her what she was going to read over the weekend. She said she would read chapters 2, 3, and 4. I proceeded to tell her that she was a good reader, and that she could read much more. I told her I wanted her to finish the book she was reading, and I gave her another Goosebumps book for her to read by Monday.

She was shocked! Her face lit up and she exclaimed, "Are you crazy? I can't finish this book and read a whole other book!" I smiled and asked her to calm down. I reiterated that she just read a page to me and was an excellent reader. Then I simply said, 'Tanesha, I just want you to read as much as you can. If you can't finish the book, that is OK. You have proven to me that you are a good reader, and I know that you can read these two books. Try to read as much as you can."

I left it at that, she walked away mumbling. Monday morning, I was in the library and Tanesha walked in at 7:45 with a huge smile on her face. She handed me the two Goosebumps books and said, "Guess what? I finished both books!"

I was thrilled for her and I could tell she was very proud of herself. I complimented her and praised her accomplishment. Then I smiled back at her and said, "OK Tanesha, here is another book for you to start and finish by tomorrow." She looked at me and rolled her eyes and said, "Oh brother!"

A Book a Day

Tanesha took the book and walked back to her class. I knew I had her hooked. For the next few weeks, she actually read a book a day. After a couple of weeks of Goosebumps, I encouraged her to read other books. But she was clearly focused on Goosebumps—she did, however, move to the next level of Goosebumps, the Fear Street series. After about a week of my trying to convince her to try Judy Blume books, she finally gave in and was pleasantly surprised. I realized it was not easy to convince her to try other books; she did it only because I asked her as a special request (and I didn't give up).

Gradually, she started to read books that I had recommended (*Tales of a Fourth Grade Nothing* and *Superfudge*, by Judy Blume, and *Roll of Thunder, Hear my Cry*, by Mildred Taylor).

Tanesha became one of the top readers of the 200 students in the summer session, and read more than 40 books. On the last day of summer school, her teacher told me that Tanesha went up to her and said she was going to sue the school and the teachers. The teacher was very surprised and asked her why. Tanesha answered, "Because my eyes hurt. I have never, ever read so much in my whole life!" She was, of course, joking, but also half-serious. She really felt she had done nothing but read, read, read all summer.

After some encouragement, Tanesha became a dedicated Goosebumps reader, and gradually started reading other authors.

Overall, she was very pleased with herself, and she was very surprised that reading could actually be fun. She said she planned to do a lot more reading during the rest of the summer and during school the following year.

When Does Encouragement Work?

There are two kinds of encouragement of reading. We can encourage children to read more, and we can encourage those who are already reading to read specific books. The cases of successful encouragement from *Voices of Readers* were cases of encouraging reading specific books. Tanesha falls into both categories. At first, Fay succeeded in encouraging her to read more. Then she encouraged her to broaden her reading.

Tanesha's case demonstrates that direct encouragement, even fairly forceful encouragement, can work to achieve both goals. Will it work in all cases? From Tanesha's case, as well as the ones we briefly surveyed at the start of this chapter, we can provisionally conclude that several conditions need to be met for encouragement to work:

1. *There needs to be access to plenty of books.* This is not a trivial condition. As we saw in Chapter 1, research shows that children of poverty have very little access to books at home, at school, and in their communities. Reading campaigns that exhort children of poverty to read more appear to have ignored this essential fact. Thanks to the The Summer Reading Program, Tanesha had access to plenty of books.

2. *The reading that is suggested must be extremely compelling.* To help guarantee that this will happen, the teacher or librarian needs to have some understanding of the child's interests coupled with a knowledge of what is available; Fay encouraged

Tanesha to read two of the most popular children's authors, R.L. Stine and Judy Blume, expanding her reading of the first and starting to read the second. But Fay knew enough about Tanesha to realize that she would enjoy these books. Miss B., in example (4), knew the child's interests and knew what books were available on this topic. Greaney and Hagerty's fifth graders did not, apparently, profit from their parents' encouragement to read the newspaper because they found the newspaper dull.

3. *The student is capable of doing the reading, but lacks confidence.* Tanesha was clearly capable of doing the reading. Fay made sure this was the case before she intervened. Tanesha, however, did not realize that she could read so much and enjoy it so much.

4. *The student still has free choice and suggestions are made only occasionally.* Tanesha had the choice of not taking the recommendations, and there was no attempt to control most of her reading. There was no "extreme pressure" of the kind one reader experienced (example 5); rather, successful interventions were "occasional suggestions" (example 2).

Successful encouragement of reading requires access to lots of compelling and comprehensible reading and free choice.

Carlsen and Sherrill come to a reasonable conclusion: "Educators such as the 'Bo-Peep' teacher who 'leaves them alone' and the 'Old Woman in the Shoe' teacher who 'whips them all soundly' may equally discourage and frustrate student enthusiasm for reading" (p. 143). Simply making books available will be enough for many students, especially those who are already readers, but some will profit from encouragement and from suggestions. Encouragement, however, does not mean forced reading: It appears to work best when students have the ability to read certain texts but need encouragement, when they are unaware of what is available, when the texts are right for them, and they still have a choice of what they read.[3]

Returning to Library Latchkey Children

Back in Chapter 1, we told you about library latchkey children, children whose parents left them in the public library after school for several hours every day. Researcher Sam Pack observed these children and found that some of them, despite being surrounded by books, did not read but just "hung out" and socialized. We have nothing against children enjoying each other's company, but it is sad that the children took no advantage whatsoever of this ready supply of reading. It is also sad that no librarian was able to encourage them to read. Some "occasional suggestions," based on the boys' interests, might have made a huge difference.

Lowering Our Standards

We have concluded from our experiences that we need to take condition (2) very seriously: The books we recommend need to be truly interesting, truly compelling. And what adults think is appropriate reading is not always what children want to read. Researcher Joanne Ujiie has demonstrated this: She studied what books children said had first stimulated their interest in reading (what Jim Trelease calls a "home run" book); Missing from the list were the award winners, those books for children and adolescents that adults feel is fine literature. Rather, the children mentioned Goosebumps, *Captain Underpants, Chicka Chicka Boom Boom,* and other "lesser lights."[4]

Award-winning books are not usually very popular among children.

We therefore loaded up on Goosebumps, comic books, and other "light" reading. This was based on our own experiences. But it was the right decision: The children loved them, and as we have seen, this light reading led to "heavier" reading.

Again, the experience of Carlsen and Sherrill's subjects agree with our experiences: Several of their subjects talk about how premature exposure to "classic" and "quality" literature turned them off to reading. We already saw an example of this earlier, example (5), the case of the librarian who insisted that children read *The Last of the Mohicans.* Here are some others:

> The librarian was a sharp tongued ogre whose mere glance threatened my mental health, and being the sensitive, rather insecure child that I was, I found it less traumatic to frequent places other than the library. If a book we wanted to check out didn't suit her fancy, she would read us the riot act with her brows furrowed and her jowls drooping. And consequently, we were actually afraid to try out new types of reading or books we wanted to read because of natural inquisitiveness. (p. 115)

> When I was graduated from college I found it difficult to read anything pleasurable for almost two years. I don't really know why as I had always loved to read, but I think it might have had something to do with the fact that every time we brought up popular titles in English courses, they were ridiculed as trash and I somehow felt without realizing it that an English major only read certain books, that I was tired of reading those books and I therefore read nothing at all (p. 25).[5]

"Light reading" provides the competence that makes "heavier" reading possible.

We need, however, to remind readers that our goal is not to produce light readers for life. Although we all continue to do light reading,[6] our ultimate goal is to help children develop the competence to read truly demanding literature. Goosebumps is a bridge. Our intention is to supply this link missing from the lives of many children.

Joining the Literacy Club

Frank Smith, in his book *Joining the Literacy Club,* argues that reading is not enough.[7] To acquire the conventions of writing and attain high levels of literacy,

*Joining the
"literacy club"
results in full
acquisition of the
conventions of
writing.*

children also need to become members of the "literacy club," that is, they need to consider themselves to be the kinds of people who read and write. When children become members of the literacy club, or even consider themselves to be potential members, they then automatically and subconsciously absorb the conventions of writing as they read, the same way members of other clubs absorb the characteristics of the clubs they join. Athletes, for example, acquire not only the physical skills they need to play their sport, but also pick up the nonfunctional traits and mannerisms of other players.

How do you join? You are invited in by a member of the club, when, as Frank Smith expresses it, somebody makes it clear that "you are one of us." We regard the one-on-one conferences as a potential means of inviting children into the literacy club. This happened, we believe, with Jimmy:

Jimmy was a middle school student but far behind his peers in reading. In fact, after the first conference, it was clear that Jimmy could hardly read at all.

Fay noted that during the core reading/literature time, Jimmy would stare at the walls because he could not follow along with the class. The reason for this became evident when Jimmy was discovered reading *Sports Illustrated*, a magazine written at a fairly demanding level. During his first conference, Jimmy said he had read an article on Barry Bonds. It was, however, obvious that he hadn't when the teacher asked him questions and then asked him to read it to her.

Fay encouraged Jimmy to do his own independent reading during the literature time; when the class was reading and discussing *Where the Red Fern Grows*, Jimmy was reading books at the first grade level. When the teacher worked with him during conferencing, Jimmy was given the individualized attention he needed, which included some direct work on "skills," but the focus was primarily on helping Jimmy select books that were appropriate for him.

After this happened, Jimmy's attitude changed tremendously. He no longer had to "fake it" but could actually read. Jimmy didn't mind reading "easy" books, because it was the first time he could actually read something. The social implications of what he was reading were simply not important to him. What was important was that he felt good about what he was reading, and he was excited about the content of the books he was reading, books about sports and animals, in addition to children's literature. It was amazing to see his confidence increase as the weeks went by.

During his entire school career, Jimmy did very little homework: The material was too difficult and he had no one at home to help him. Now, for the first time in his school career, Jimmy was actually doing his homework, reading and rereading the books his teacher gave him; he told us that he knew the teacher would talk to him about what he read, and this was a tremendous incentive. (Jimmy told us that he didn't consider the reading as homework, just as reading.)

We attribute Jimmy's shift in attitude and his "joining the literacy club" to the one-on-one conferences, and a careful and caring teacher who took the trouble to find reading material that was appropriate for him and who took a real interest in what he was reading.

We have no doubt that given access to interesting and comprehensible books, Jimmy will eventually become a very competent member of the literacy club.

Eve Marin, one of our teachers, said in her notes that she found "daily interviewing" of the students "a helpful and important part of the program." She said that the students "knew I would be asking them how much they had read and would question them on what they had read. In fact, they wanted to be interviewed. They loved the attention . . . I found it refreshing that the students actually wanted to do the work." Eve Marin invited her students into the literacy club.

Thanks to conferencing, Jimmy joined the literacy club and became a reader.

One More Summer Reading Study

If we were doing a "proper" survey of the literature, we would have included this study in the first chapter, but we decided that it fit here much better, now that we

Helen Aason made heroic efforts to involve the school library, public library, and parents to surround students with books of interest to them during the summer.

have discussed the role of encouragement and when encouragement can help. This study was published in 1959, but the author, Helen Aason, was quite aware of the drop in reading one sees after summer break: "Like other classroom teachers, I know full well what can happen to reading skills when children do not open a book from the time school closes in June till school bells ring again in September" (p. 353).[8]

Aason encouraged two classes of fourth graders (64 students) to read over the summer in a variety of ways. Just before the summer break began, she and the students discussed "various kinds of books they might like to read and the importance of selecting books that were not too difficult" (p. 354). She went to the trouble of preparing a reading list of 35 books, but based it on a survey she did of the children's own reading preferences. When she handed out the survey, she showed copies of each book to the children "and reviewed each briefly as I held it up. If a book appealed to a child, he checked it on his list to remind him to read it during the summer" (p. 354).

Aason took advantage of both the school and public libraries. Before the school year ended, she and the school librarian organized a school library "browsing day." The school librarian arranged an attractive display of books and provided the children with an orientation to the library. The local public librarian visited the classes, bringing samples of the newest and most interesting books, and Aason made sure each child had a library card. In addition, children were told about a bookmobile that came to the community every week.

Aason also enlisted the help of the parents, urging them to surround the children with good books, go with them to the public library, read to them, and discuss books with them.

The children were not required to write book reports; rather, they kept a record of the books they read as well as the number of pages read.

Aason tested the children at the beginning and end of the summer, using the Stanford Reading Achievement test. She held individual conferences with each student before the vacation began. Each was told what their standardized test score was in reading and what the score meant: "This information alone created intense interest in the program and kindled a desire to make gains in reading during the summer" (p. 354). The test scores of the readers were compared with those of a comparison class, 32 fourth graders with similar backgrounds and similar IQ scores.

Aason's readers gained seven months on a standardized test of reading over the summer.

The results were impressive. The comparison students read at the 5.2 grade level at the beginning of the summer, and made no progress at all over the summer, getting the same score when the test was administered again in September. The readers, however, improved from 5.4 in the spring to 6.1 in the fall, a gain of seven months in three months time. (One of the children grew a spectacular 3.5 years! We recalculated the gains for the children in the reading classes without this child's score, just in case there was an error in the scoring—the gain without this "outlier" was still a very impressive 6.6 months.) Aason also informs us that about two-thirds of the children in the two reading classes improved over the summer, but only one-third of the comparison children gained.

Aason clearly provided what we called "direct encouragement," and did so in a way that met all the conditions for encouragement to succeed. We review each one and show how Aason did it:

Condition 1: There needs to be access to plenty of books. These children were middle class, so they came from print-rich environments; in addition, as described, the teacher made tremendous efforts to introduce them to the school and public library.

Condition 2: The reading that is suggested must be extremely compelling. Aason cleverly made sure this condition was met, with her survey, her reading list based on the survey, and the expert help of school and public librarians.

Condition 3: The student is capable of doing the reading, but lacks confidence. Aason made sure that the books were within the students' abilities, and did not push them into "hard" reading.

Condition 4: The student still has free choice and suggestions are made only occasionally. Aason provided a list, and she and librarians made recommendations, but the choice was up to the students.

It is also highly likely that Ms. Aason invited these children into the literacy club.

Some Final Observations

We close with both a word of caution about the limitations of our results, expressed in the usual careful way scholars like to say these things. We then suggest that our results might apply to more than just summer programs.

A Limitation

An obvious limitation of this study is that it dealt with a specific population of students reading a limited range of reading material. Although our results are consistent with those found in other studies, it is important that the results be replicated with other groups, and with other reading material.

Our results apply to more than just summer: They confirm that access to interesting reading and encouraging reading is important year–round.

More than Summertime

We hope we have provided an effective alternative to the usual summer reading camp, and have provided a means of helping children "close the gap" over the summer. But we think that our results tell us much more than that.

Our experience confirms the importance of providing access to print and access to interesting reading material. For many of our students, this was enough. While Barbara Heyns and Jimmy Kim showed us that more access to reading over the summer (proximity to libraries) results in more reading, we wanted to see what would happen if we brought the reading to the students. If, as the research reviewed in Chapter 1 suggested, "reluctant readers" are to a great extent children who have little access to books, would providing the books result in enthusiastic readers? The results, as we have seen, were very positive.

We have also confirmed that students can make impressive progress in literacy without massive amounts of direct instruction, without endless and dull workbooks and vocabulary lists. We have confirmed that the most effective way is also the most pleasant way.

A clear advantage to doing a free reading program over the summer is that summer programs are not subject to the same constraints as the curriculum during the school year. At the time of this writing, curricula in language arts and reading in the United States has become extremely rigid. Teachers have little room to experiment and try other options. Summer is the ideal time to try something different.

Our hope, however, is that our results will help change all this, that they will encourage a move away from the inflexible curricula that are now in use. If a program such as The Summer Reading Program works during the summer, it will work all year long.

Finally, our results provide, we think, strong support for the importance of libraries, both school and public libraries during the school year, and public libraries open during the summer, open during the day, in the evening, and on weekends, with quality collections of children's and adolescent literature. Not every community will be able to set up a Summer Reading Program, but every community will, we hope, be able to offer all children a plentiful supply of interesting reading material.

Our results confirm that students can improve in reading just by reading books they find interesting.

Our results strongly confirm the importance of libraries.

*N*OTES

1. G. Robert Carlsen and Anne Sherrill, *Voices of Readers: How We Come to Love Books* (Urbana, IL: NCTE, 1988).
2. Vincent Greaney and Mary Hegarty, Correlations of leisure time reading. *Journal of Research in Reading* 10(1)(1987), 3–20.
3. We suspect that direct encouragement was a crucial factor with Paul as well, a boy who read over 40 Goosebumps books over the summer and clearly enjoyed them. When first asked why he read so much, he responded that he didn't know. With additional probing, he said he read because he had nothing else to do, because he was able to take books and magazines home, and also because his teacher told him to. Paul received no support or encouragement from his parents for his reading, and it is likely that he had no other source of books, a sad commentary. Increased access and teacher encouragement combined to create a dedicated reader.

   According to Neuman and Celano (2006), the "leave them alone" strategy may be more common among lower socioeconomic status groups. They observed that preschool children from low-income families "received little direction" (p. 192) in the public library. They often entered the preschool area of the library by themselves, with a peer, "but rarely with an adult. With little to do they would wander in and wander out" (p. 191), spent little time with books, and would rarely leave with a book checked out. But "for children from middle-income neighborhoods, activities were highly focused. Invariably, the accompanying adult took charge" (p. 191). The adult would suggest books, and steered children to appropriate books at their level; . . . without exception, [the visits] ended with checkouts of books, and often, videos" (p. 191). Neuman and Celano suggest that librarians may be able to play this role for children from low-income families. Susan Neuman and Donna Celano, The knowledge gap: Implications of leveling the playing field for low-income and middle-income children. *Reading Research Quarterly* 41(2)(2006), 176–201.

4. Joanne Ujiie and Stephen Krashen, Home run books and reading enjoyment. *Knowledge Quest* 3(1)(2002), 36–37; Jim Trelease, in *The Read-Aloud Handbook,* suggested that a single positive experience with a good book can create a lifetime reader. He used the term *home run book,* inspired by a passage from Fadiman's *The Overall Boys:* "One's first book, kiss, home run, is always the best." Several studies have confirmed that Trelease is right: A very large percentage (well over half) of elementary school children agreed that there was one book that interested them in reading, and they were easily able to name the book, a result confirmed in Christy Lao's research. Jim Trelease, *The Read-Aloud Handbook,* 5th ed. (New York: Penguin, 2001); Clifton Fadiman, *Party of One: The Selected Writings of Clifton Fadiman* (Cleveland, OH: The World Publishing Company, 1947). For studies of the home run book experience, see Ujiie and Krashen (2002), and Debra Von Sprecken, JiYoung Kim, and Stephen Krashen, The home run book: Can one positive reading experience create a reader? *California School Library Journal* 23(2)(2000), 8–9; Christy Lao, Prospective teachers' journey to becoming readers. *New Mexico Journal of Reading* 32(2)(2003), 14–20.

5. Victor Nell questions the entire idea of a "classic." His studies show that judgments of the quality of literature are highly correlated with how difficult texts are to read! Victor Nell, *Lost in a Book* (New Haven, CT: Yale University Press, 1988).

6. Janice Pilgreen and Karen Russikoff, Shaking the tree of "forbidden fruit": A study of light reading. *Reading Improvement* 31(2)(1994), 122–23.

7. Frank Smith, *Joining the Literacy Club* (Portsmouth, NH: Heinemann, 1988).

8. Helen Aason, A summer's growth in reader. *Elementary School Journal* 60(1959), 70–74.

Individual Conference and Reading Logs

1. Each student should have a folder.

2. The TEACHER keeps the folders in a box or file cabinet. Students do NOT keep these folders.

3. After the folder is used or student has met with the teacher, it should be *placed at the bottom of the stack* to ensure that all students have an equal opportunity to meet with the teacher.

4. During the conferencing time, students are to meet with the teacher *one-on-one*. This should not be done in small groups.

5. During the conferencing time, teachers have the opportunity to get to know the student's specific reading skills and interests. Some examples are:

   a. Discuss what they are reading. For example, ask them what they think about the main character, the book, etc.

   b. Have students read aloud. Students usually love to read to the teacher!

6. Under the section of "comments, readings, and assignments" teachers should *write as much as they want,* and *whatever they want* to. Some suggestions to write:

   a. What the student has read the day before (or since the last meeting).

   b. Comments on student's progress.

c. Specific reading assignment or agreement (for example, "Lisa promises to read two chapters tonight.").

d. Paraprofessionals, tutors, or other support staff who conference with the child (or read with them individually) should also fill out or note that they met with the child.

e. Comments on what types of books the student likes. Favorite topics, hobbies, etc. should be noted.

Student Conferences Reading Log

Student's Name _____

Date	Title	Comments, Readings, Assignments	Teacher Signature

Book Record

....

Student's Name _____ **Date** _____

Title _____

Author _____ **Genre** _____

I would rate this book (circle one number):

1	2	3	4	5	6	7	8	9	10

Awful   OK   Excellent

☹   ☺

Comments or thoughts (optional):

Teacher's Signature _____

Recommended Checklist and Components of an Independent Reading Program

_____ 1. *NO book reports!* No tests or quizzes!

_____ 2. Provide a *variety of reading materials.* This includes books, magazines, comic books, newspapers. *Note:* Make sure there are plenty of reading materials that are above and below the students' grade levels.

_____ 3. Provide students with *access to books.* Remember, not all students have access to books! Oftentimes the school library has limited access for students (once-a-week visits are not enough!). Providing your students with enough books for everyone is important.

_____ 4. Think of *creative ways to get more books* or reading materials in your classroom. Garage sales, used bookstores, and classroom book orders (Scholastic, etc.) are some inexpensive ways to purchase reading materials. Also ask your friends for old magazines and books. Have fundraisers for building your classroom library. Look into other sources such as local businesses.

_____ 5. Display/Classroom library. It should *look inviting* (think of bookstores!). Students

88

APPENDIX B

*Recommended
Checklist and
Components of
an Independent
Reading Program*

should be *able to check out reading materials daily.*

_____ 6. Provide *daily reading time.* Remember, this is not homework or studying time!

_____ 7. Classroom reading environment. Students should be *able to read wherever they want to in the classroom.* Allow for comfortable reading places (rugs, pillows, etc.). Let students read next to their friends, under the desk, on top of the back counter.

_____ 8. Room should be *silent during SSR time.* Let students share or talk about their reading during a specified time (for example, a few minutes before or after SSR time).

_____ 9. Allow students to *choose* what they want to read.

_____ 10. *Staff training.* Teachers should have information on the importance of SSR and how to implement a successful SSR program.

_____ 11. *Supportive administration.* A supportive administration will provide teachers/classrooms with more access to books and monies to go toward classroom libraries.

_____ 12. *Encourage and motivate* your students to read outside of school! Teach them to LOVE reading.

Access

By far the most important component of an indepen-dent reading program is access to books. As we saw in Chapter 1, more access means more reading, and chil-dren of poverty have very little access to books. We must constantly remind ourselves that for many chil-dren, school is the only place they can find interesting and comprehensible reading material.

Unfortunately, in many schools children are given limited access to the school library (once-a-week visits are not enough); this puts a bigger burden on the teacher.

Variety

In Chapter 3, we discussed Jim Trelease's idea that sometimes one positive reading experience, a "home run" book, is enough to create a lifelong reading habit. In Joanne Ujiie's home run book study (for details, see page 81, note 4), children were asked to name their home run book. The list was huge. The children named a wide variety of titles. We interpret this as showing that we need to include a wide variety of book titles in our school library and classroom library collections; we cannot predict what book will be a home run book for each child. And, of course, the home run reading ex-perience could be a comic book or a magazine.

Include Light Reading

We are firm believers in light reading. Our goal in en-couraging light reading is not to encourage a lifetime diet of only junk reading; rather, it is clear that light reading serves as a conduit for heavier reading; it is an important bridge that builds reading ability and vocabulary, and makes more challenging reading possible. Sadly, many children do not have access to light reading; we feel it is our job to make sure they do.

APPENDIX B

*Recommended
Checklist and
Components of
an Independent
Reading Program*

Jo Worthy and her associates at the University of Texas at Austin first asked sixth graders in the Austin area what they liked to read. The most popular categories, by far, were scary stories and comic books. She then did a survey of school and classroom libraries in the Austin area. In school libraries comics were "largely unavailable" and scary books were only "moderately available." Classroom libraries also had very little of this kind of reading.[1]

Parents of children in high-income families can easily afford this kind of reading; children from low-income families are dependent on libraries, and unfortunately, libraries don't have what they really want to read.

Above and Below Level

The current trend is to restrict reading to the student's reading level, which is determined by testing the child. A child who reads at the fourth-grade level is allowed to read books only at that level. The level of a book is determined by mechanical formulae based on factors, such as average sentence length, and whether frequently used words appear in the text.

We don't think this is necessary. There is a much easier way for readers to select texts: Are they comprehensible and interesting? It doesn't take long for a reader to determine this. All it takes is sampling a little of the text (reading it).

If a child needs help, we feel that teachers and librarians, people who know the children and know children's literature, are much better at providing it than a reading test and a reading formula.

Restricting the range of reading, in fact, could be harmful. While children may select easy books for free reading, they often select books that are above their "official" level.[2]

Also, reading easy books is not a waste of time. It may be that the lighter reading we are denying readers contains text that could be meaningful and important to the reader. Kathleen Sespaukas has pointed out to us that easy books may contain sections well above their indicated level, that is, a book considered to be at the fourth-grade level may contain quite a bit of material at the fifth- and sixth-grade level. Reading level is an average and this average does not apply to every sentence. In addition, easy reading may help readers get started in an unfamiliar topic or genre. Betty Carter points out that librarians frequently suggest that adults read books written for younger readers when dealing with unfamiliar material. This reading builds background knowledge that makes subsequent reading more comprehensible.[3]

They Don't Have to Finish Every Book They Start

One of the behaviors that distinguishes good readers is their willingness to abandon a book that they do not enjoy or that is too challenging.

—Linda Lamme[4]

Susan Ohanian has observed that, "Lousy readers don't start books because they're scared they'll be stuck with them forever" (p. 123). They think that once they start reading a book, they have to finish it. We think that one of the attributes of an excellent reader is knowing that you don't have to finish every book you start to read! Recreational reading is, after all, recreational. If the book isn't right, isn't interesting, isn't comprehensible, good readers put it down and try something else.[5]

When NOT to Do Independent Reading

Some people think that independent reading programs should be done at the same time every day, schoolwide: At a certain time, such as between 10 and 10:15 a.m., everything stops, and everyone "drops

92

APPENDIX B

*Recommended
Checklist and
Components of
an Independent
Reading Program*

everything and reads." Students read, teachers read, administrators read, support staff reads, and even visitors to the school stop and read.

There are problems with this, however. A study published in 1980 tells us why. Researcher Marilyn Joy Minton reported on the effectiveness of a sustained silent reading (SSR) program done for 15 minutes per day over a semester for ninth graders in a high school in the San Diego area. SSR flopped. Gains in reading achievement were tiny, and attitudes toward reading got worse. In fact, fewer students were reading a book at the end of the semester than at the beginning!

One of the things that went wrong was the fact that the program "was based on the belief that everyone can and should read at the same time" (p. 502). Insisting that everyone read at the same time meant that SSR took place during classes, such as industrial arts and physical education, classes in which there was no place to sit and read comfortably and classes in which few or no books were available. Minton's reasonable conclusion is that "if an SSR program is to encompass all students, the circumstances must be carefully selected" (p. 502). (There were other problems with this SSR program, and we will discuss them later.)[6]

Another case in which SSR apparently flopped was reported by Florences Maynes in 1981. Adding 45 minutes of SSR for four days a week did not result in additional gains over a comparison group for readers in grades 2 through 6 in a school in Ontario. But the extra reading took place during the children's lunch period! Maynes tells us that the children's interest in reading did not differ from the comparison students, but we are amazed it didn't get worse.[7]

Comfort and Quiet

Students read more when they have a quiet, comfortable place to read.[8] We need to make sure that the environment for classroom reading is comfortable and quiet.

Students do not have to sit at their desks when they read. Ideally, easy chairs, pillows, and comfortable rugs should be available. Students should be able to read wherever they want to in the classroom. They should, in other words, have the same rights as pleasure readers as we do.

The room should be quiet. We recognize the importance of students being able to discuss their reading and share their enthusiasm with others, but there must be some time each day when they can read in absolute silence and be undisturbed by others. Just as we did during the Summer Reading Program, we suggest scheduling a separate time for discussion and sharing.

A Little Each Day, Not All at Once

A common question asked about in-school free reading programs is whether it is better to let children read for an extended time one or two times a week, or a little each day. In the Summer Reading Program, we had the luxury of doing both at once-students read for an extended period of time every day. But this is of course not possible during the regular school year.

There has been no research that we know of dealing with this question. From our own observations, and from talking with practitioners, when time is limited and we must decide between a little each day or all at once one day a week, we tentatively come down on the side of a little each day, or what is called distributed, rather than massed, time periods. The value of independent in-school reading comes not only from the actual time spent reading but from the fact that it stimulates additional reading outside of school. Brief reading periods might be just the right thing for reluctant readers to get a taste of reading, and then want more. Our mission is achieved when the child who has resisted reading for weeks or even months suddenly says, when reading time is over, "Wait, I want to finish this part . . ."

Self-Selection

A crucial component of in-school free reading programs is self-selection. Students choose what they want to read. We need, however, to qualify this: We are not saying "anything goes."

First, not all reading in school should be selected by the student. We are not advocating a free reading-only policy. In literature classes, teachers, experts in children's and adolescent literature, assign books and recommend books. (We know, however, that a literature program is working when students read more on their own.)

Second, we do not believe in complete free choice. The content of some reading material is clearly inappropriate for free reading in school. While we would probably draw the line more liberally than most people, the line must still be drawn.

We agree with Jim Trelease, who notes that those who object to children reading certain books in school "have a right to protest and a right to be heard. What they don't have is the right to impose their will on others. In a nation governed by 'majority rules,' they have only the right to persuade the majority toward their point of view . . . Since there is not always universal agreement on what hurts and what helps children, conflicts arise. A book that might be appropriate for ninth-graders might be very inappropriate for third-graders." Trelease's solution: "[D]istricts should have clearly defined censorship policies in place, defining a board to hear the complaint, read the offending book, and make a decision on its appropriateness."[9]

Display

Jim Trelease makes a fascinating comparison between supermarkets and libraries. Supermarkets, Trelease points out, have carefully studied how to encourage customers to buy. In a nutshell, display is crucial.

Food companies pay extra to have their goods placed in the best locations: fifteen degrees below eye level is optimal, with the items face-out; specialty items sell best when placed near the checkout line, and, of course, supermarkets generally put the milk in the back of the store so people have to walk through the entire store to get to it. The more they see, the more they buy.

Trelease suggests libraries should also think carefully about display. Books should be presented face-out and new items placed near the checkout desk. Librarians need to think of ways to ensure students see more books.

Trelease notes that supermarket research shows that a large percentage of customers did not have a complete shopping list when entering the market. The same, he suggests, is probably true of visitors to libraries-display, therefore, is very important in wooing these uncommitted readers.[10]

Daily Access

Jim Trelease makes the obvious but profound and neglected pointed that "the most cost effective way of lifting circulation and reading scores" could simply be increasing trips to the library. He describes the case of one school in Texas, the Tatum Primary School.

Library visits were increased from once a week to unlimited, and the maximum number of books that could be taken out was increased from two to then. The result was a doubling of circulation. We concur that daily access to school and classroom libraries, with the abiity to take out books every day, is essential.[11]

Don't Expect Results Overnight

It takes some time for the effects of a recreational reading program to become obvious. As we stated in Chapter 1, sustained silent reading programs produce more positive results when they last for a year or longer. (The Summer Reading Program produced splendid results in just six weeks because, we think, of

APPENDIX B

*Recommended
Checklist and
Components of
an Independent
Reading Program*

the extra encouragement children received, and because so much daily reading time was available; SSR programs typically allow only ten to fifteen minutes per day.

There are good reasons why this is so: First, it takes some time for many children to find a book and settle into a reading habit. Second, the language acquisition process is not immediate. Readers need to see new words and structures several times before they are fully acquired.

There is, however, no short cut, no way of rushing progress. And there is no hurry! Once students have their home run book experience, once they become dedicated pleasure readers, if books are available to them improvement will follow. You will see gradual improvement in their reading, writing, grammar, spelling, and vocabulary, and they will easily move to higher levels of literacy.

Inform Colleagues

Back to the previous discussion of Marilyn Joy Minton's study: Another reason the study flopped was because teachers had not received much information about sustained silent reading and the program was imposed on the staff without discussion. It is crucial that teachers have information on the importance and effectiveness of SSR, know how to implement a successful SSR program, and be willing participants. It is important that teachers be enthusiastic, and that the students feel their enthusiasm.

The Administration

We have heard stories of administrators who did not understand the power of recreational reading, and who accused teachers of simply "taking it easy" during SSR time, avoiding the serious hard work of teaching. We have also heard stories of administrators who strongly support SSR and make heroic efforts to provide additional books for children and to increase funding for libraries.

Administrators need to be informed. They need to know that when students are reading for pleasure, they are gaining in reading ability, writing ability, grammar, vocabulary, and spelling, and increasing their general knowledge. They need to know that although free reading is pleasant, is it also serious. And they will be pleased to know that free reading is an excellent means of raising reading test scores.

*N*OTES

1. Jo Worthy, Megan Moorman, and Margo Turner, What Johnny likes to read is hard to find in school. *Reading Research Quarterly* 34(10)(1999), 12–27.

2. Vera Southgate, Helen Arnold, and Sandra Johnson, *Extending Beginning Reading* (London: Heinemann Educational Books, 1981).

3. Betty Carter, Formula for failure. *School Library Journal,* July 1, 2000.

4. Linda Lamme, A children's literature expert speaks: A literature perspective on accelerated reader. *Journal of Children's Literature* 29(2)(2003), 37–45.

5. Susan Ohanian, *Who's in Charge? A Teacher Speaks Her Mind* (Portsmouth, NH: Heinemann, 1994).

6. Marilyn Joy Minton, The effect of sustained silent reading upon comprehension and attitudes among ninth graders. *Journal of Reading* 23(1980): 498–502.

7. Florence Maynes, Uninterrupted sustained silent reading. *Reading Research Quarterly* 17(1) (1981), 159–60.

8. Stephen Krashen, *The Power of Reading,* 2d ed (Bridgeport, CT: Libraries Unlimited, 2004).

9. Jim Trelease, *Censorship and Children's Books.* Online. June 7, 2004, www.trelease-on-reading.com/censor _entry.html.

10. Jim Trelease, *The Read Aloud Handbook,* ch 6 (New York: Penguin, 2001).

11. Ibid, ch 5.

Sophia's Choice: Summer Reading*

Shu-Yuan Lin, Fay Shin, and Stephen Krashen

I really enjoy reading when there are no strings attached, when there is no book report or assignment . . . . I also like the freedom of choosing any book I wish to read. . . . I believe that people would read a lot more if they find books they are fascinated by. No pressure of doing well on an assignment, but the pleasure of reading . . . I know when I find a book I like. I just can't put it aside. On the other hand, when I am being forced to read, I lose interest instantly.

—Sophia

Sophia is the teenage daughter in a family of middle-class immigrants from Taiwan. The family arrived in the United States when Sophia was in grade 6; at the time she had only minimal English, the result of private lessons several days per week for two years.

After entering grade 8, Sophia was tested in English reading on the Idaho Standards Achievement Test (ISAT) each year in the fall and in the spring. At first glance, things don't look good: As shown in Table A.1, Sophia's scores actually drop each year. She dropped

*Published in *Knowledge Quest* 35(4)(2007).

Table A.1

Sophia's Decline during the School Year

Academic Year	Drop in Percentile
Grade 8: '02–'03	29
Grade 9: '03–'04	21
Grade 10: '04–'05	21

29 percentiles during grade 8, 21 percentiles during grade 9, and another 21 percentiles during grade 10. It seems that Sophia was falling behind her classmates each year, a student who was clearly in trouble.

But Sophia was not in trouble. At the start of grade 8, she scored at the fifty-third percentile (see Table A.2), a remarkable achievement for someone who had only been in the United States for two years. The ISAT is required from grades 2 to 10, but if students achieve scores at the "proficient" level at grade 10, they need not take the test again. Sophia reached this level.

Table A.2

Sophia's Percentile Rankings

Academic Year	Percentile
Grade 8: '02–'03	53 > 24
Grade 9: '03–'04	75 > 54
Grade 10: '04–'05	68 > 47
	fall > spring

Since tenth grade, Sophia has been a member of the National Honor Society. Last year, she was selected as the outstanding junior year debater, even though it was her first year participating in debate. At the time of this writing, Sophia is in grade 12. She is enrolled, and is doing "A" work in a college level English class, and achieved a perfect score on the placement examination required for enrollment.

Table A.3 explains the mystery. It is a rearrangement of Sophia's scores to reflect what happened over the summer; each summer, Sophia made substantial gains in reading, making up for what she had lost during the academic year, or more.

What did Sophia do over the summer? Did she attend special classes, getting instruction in reading strategies and meta-cognition? Did she work through massive amounts of vocabulary lists? Did she read under a strict regimen, applying grim determination to working through a list of required books, completing book reports and summaries? The answer: None of the above. All she did was read for pleasure: No book reports, no "related reading activities," and all her reading was self-selected.

According to her mother, Sophia read an average of about fifty books per summer. Early favorites were the Nancy Drew and Sweet Valley High series, and Sophia then moved on to the Christy Miller series and

Table A.3

Sophia's Summer Gains

Summer	Percentile
8–9: ('03)	24 > 75
9–10: ('04)	54 > 68
	spring > fall

other books by Francine Pascal, the author of the Sweet Valley series. (Sophia informed us that she was "addicted" to the Christy Miller books; it took her only a week to read the entire series "because I just couldn't put them down.")

Her choices thus concur with research showing that series books are enormously popular among young readers (Krashen and Ujiie, 2005) and with arguments that "narrow reading" is a very efficient way of building language competence, because texts are interesting and comprehensible (Krashen, 2004).

This is a startling result, but it is not new. Sophia's experience is precisely what was reported by Barbara Heyns in 1975, who showed that the difference in reading development between children from low and middle income families is because of what happens over the summer: Both groups make similar gains during the year, but children from high income families improve over the summer, while those from low-income families either stay the same or get worse. Over the years, the difference builds up until it becomes very large (Entwisle, Alexander, and Olson, 1997).

What Happens Over the Summer?

What happens over the summer that makes such a difference? Access to books and reading. Heyns found that those who live closer to libraries read more, and both Heyns (1975) and Kim (2005) found that children who read more over the summer make more gains in reading.

Of course, Sophia had an advantage that not all children have: Access to plenty of books.

The public library was the primary source for Sophia's reading. The library had a summer reading program and Sophia joined it. After finishing reading a book, she went back to check out another book. She got small prizes such as stickers as rewards but the real reward was the pleasure Sophia received from reading her self-selected books. (See Krashen, 2003, 2005 for a discussion of the lack of research on rewards for reading, as well as possible dangers.) Sophia even took the city bus with her younger brother to the public library when her mother was too busy with work to take her to the library.

Sophia is also part of a family that supports education and encourages her to read. Summer reading, encouraged by her mother, had been a regular part of Sophia's life for years. Sophia had been a pleasure reader in Mandarin before she and her family moved to the United States, and lived in a print-rich environment in Taiwan. After arriving in the United States, however, she had no access to new books in Mandarin, and had to learn to read in English to continue her pleasure reading habit. She profited, thus, from "de facto bilingual education," a good background in her first language. Her case confirms that the pleasure-reading habit transfers across languages (Kim and Cho, 2005).

Sophia's case is a good example of using resources from public libraries. The summer reading program at the public library not only motivated Sophia to read but the wide variety of reading books also attracted her to visit again and again. Not all children are so lucky, but the situation can be improved. More and better public libraries are, of course, part of the solution, especially for children who have no other sources of books.

Summer reading programs, those that emphasize lots of interesting reading and gentle encouragement, have also been shown to be extremely effective. Shin (2001) reported that her sixth graders grew a spectacular 1.3 years on the Nelson-Denny reading comprehension test, from grade level 4.0 to grade 5.4, and equaled comparisons (six months' gain) in a traditional program in vocabulary growth after only five and a half weeks in a program that included two hours of free reading each day and regular trips to the school library.

The Effect of School Reading

Rather than just work on improving book access during the summer, however, in order to allow all children to improve as Sophia did, we must ask what happens during the school year. It appears that much of what happens works against reading development.

Sophia's mother provides insight into the situation: During the school year, Sophia is so busy with school work that she has hardly any free time to read. Sophia's mother, in fact, joked that it might be a good idea to keep her daughter at home during the school year in order to increase her improvement on standardized tests of reading.

WORKS CITED

Entwisle, Doris, Karl Alexander, and Linda Olson. 1997. *Children, Schools, and Inequality.* Boulder, CO: Westview Press.

Heyns, Barbara. 1975. *Summer Learning and the Effect of School.* New York: Academic Press.

Kim, Jimmy. 2003. Summer reading and the ethnic achievement gap. *Journal of Education for Students Placed at Risk* 9(2): 169–188.

Kim, Hae-Young, and Kyung-Sook Cho. 2005. The influence of first language reading on second language reading and second language acquisition. *International Journal of Foreign Language Teaching* 1, 4: 13–16.

Krashen, Stephen. 1996. *Under Attack: The Case Against Bilingual Education.* Culver City: Language Education Associates.

Krashen, Stephen. 2003. The (lack of) experimental evidence supporting the use of accelerated reader. *Journal of Children's Literature* 29(2): 9, 16–30.

Krashen, S. 2004. *The Power of Reading.* 2nd ed. Portsmouth, NH: Heinemann and Westport, CT: Libraries Unlimited.

Krashen, Stephen. 2005. Accelerated reader: Evidence still lacking. *Knowledge Quest* 33(3): 48–49.

Krashen, Stephen, and Joanne Ujiie. 2005. Junk food is bad for you, but junk reading is good for you.

International Journal of Foreign Language Teaching 1, 3: 5–12.

Shin, Fay. 2001. Motivating students with Goosebumps and other popular books. *CSLA Journal (California School Library Association)* 25(1): 15–19.

APPENDIX C

Sophia's Choice:
Summer Reading

Index